IN THE LAND OF BREATHITT

A Guide to Breathitt County

IN THE LAND OF
BREATHITT

*Compiled by Workers of the Writers' Program
of the Work Projects Administration
in the State of Kentucky*

AMERICAN GUIDE SERIES
ILLUSTRATED

COMMONWEALTH BOOK COMPANY
St. Martin, Ohio

THE UNIVERSITY OF KENTUCKY,
STATE-WIDE SPONSOR OF THE
KENTUCKY WRITERS' PROJECT

FEDERAL WORKS AGENCY
JOHN M. CARMODY, *Administrator*

WORK PROJECTS ADMINISTRATION
HOWARD O. HUNTER, *Commissioner*
FLORENCE KERR, *Assistant Commissioner*
GEORGE H. GOODMAN, *State Administrator*

Copyright © 1941 by Breathitt County Board of Education
Copyright © 2020 by Commonwealth Book Company
All rights reserved
Printed in the United States of America

ISBN: 978-1-948986-26-7

FOREWORD

Shortly before the manuscript of this book was sent to press Breathitt County received Nation-wide newspaper, magazine, and radio attention. Once again it was "Bloody Breathitt"—the sensational Breathitt that is so well, and, perhaps, justly established in the traditions of journalism. There is, however, a Breathitt of more varied mien. The workaday world of the mountain farm and the ancient leisure that broods over woodland and stream have also fashioned the history and life of our people. Churches and especially schools have played an increasingly important part in the thoughts and actions of our youth. Times have changed and so has Breathitt.

When preparations were being made in 1938 for the centennial observance of the county's formation the following year, we took advantage of the opportunity offered by the Kentucky Writers' Project to present in book form a more balanced picture of Breathitt County. Conceived as a guide book, it has captured much of the less famed Breathitt. Early salt wells, log runs, school life in the early log schoolhouses, and the "feel" of Breathitt today have found their place among the innumerable details, episodes and interpretations that portray "The Land of Breathitt." After several unavoidable delays and painstaking effort the work undertaken as a centennial commemoration has been completed. It is inevitable that in a book of this type some facts will be questioned. Wherever this occurs it has been unintentional, for a just and accurate account has always been the first consideration. IN THE LAND OF BREATHITT is therefore offered to the citizens of the county, to tourists and to those whose curiosity is aroused by the epithet, "Bloody Breathitt," as a portrait of that *other* Breathitt.

MARIE TURNER, *Superintendent*
Breathitt County Schools.

PREFACE

When the County Superintendent of Schools at Jackson, Kentucky, requested the Kentucky Writers' Project to write a book on Breathitt, we were interested but doubtful. The mountain people, with good reason, have been more or less suspicious of outsiders seeking information, no matter in what form it is to appear. But when we were assured that the County Board of Education would cooperate with us, we agreed to prepare the book. A local research worker was assigned and in a short time material began to arrive at the State office.

LaMar Hamilton of the State Editorial Staff was sent to Jackson when the time came to begin the writing, and he stayed in the county three months gathering material and writing. He made friends with the people and won their confidence. After the manuscript was finished, parts of it were read by a number of people familiar with various aspects of the county's history and the life of its citizens. Others read the whole manuscript, and offered their suggestions and criticisms.

We are confident in presenting this book to the public that here is the balanced truth about Breathitt County. We are grateful to the following citizens for their cooperation and interest in the preparation of the manuscript and who made the writing of it by Mr. Hamilton a real pleasure: Myrtle Anderson, principal Oakdale Vocational School, Oakdale; Bertha Arrowood, teacher, Canoe; Grannis Back, lawyer, Jackson; Hiram Bach, Stevenson; Capt. A. C. Cope, Thirty-eighth Military Police Company, National Guard, Jackson; Annabelle Combs, Richmond; Tom Cope, Lexington, formerly of Jackson; David Donoho, art teacher Breathitt High School, Jackson; Mrs. G. E. Drushal, Riverside Christian Training School, Lost Creek; Dr. K. B. Daniels, Jackson; J. C. Feltner, county agricultural agent, Jackson; Mrs. O. J. Gillum, Jackson; Tom Haddix, Haddix; A. H. Hargis, former State Senator, Jackson; York M. Jackson, superintendent Highland Institute, Guerrant; Maj. R. W. Jones, superintendent Robinson Agricultural Sub-station, Quicksand; Clyde K. Landrum, teacher, Jackson; Rev. Lela G. McConnell, president Mount Carmel Association, Mount Carmel; Elizabeth E. O'Connor, president Oakdale Vocational Schools and Missions, Oakdale; John Patrick, former clerk Breathitt Circuit Court, Jackson; Frank Riffle, Jackson; H. Price Sewell, former mayor of Jackson, Jackson; Arch Smith, Jackson; Harlan Strong, Jackson; Charles Terry, Jackson; Mrs. C. P. Thacker, Jackson; Jesse E. Turner, teacher, Canoe; Marie R. Turner, county superintendent of schools, Jackson; R. M. Van Horne, principal Breathitt High School, Jackson; Dr. J. O. VanMeter, president Lees Junior College, Jackson; Galen White, Jackson.

Others, too numerous to list in the limited space of this book, supplied material and information that has added to the accuracy, detail, and color of IN THE LAND OF BREATHITT. Most of the photographs were contributed by Mr. David Donoho, art teacher Breathitt High School; a few were taken by LaMar Hamilton, author; the W.P.A., State Planning Board, and Mrs. Marie R. Turner supplied several; and the picture of Jackson around 1890 was copied from a print supplied by Dr. J. O. VanMeter, president of Lees College.

Acknowledgement is due also to U. R. Bell, former State Supervisor of the Kentucky Writers' Project, under whose leadership the book was prepared.

We take this opportunity to place on record our sincere gratitude for the contributions of all these people and regret that space does not permit the naming of many others who in various ways assisted Mr. Hamilton.

WILLIAM R. BREYER,
State Supervisor,
Kentucky Writers' Project.

CONTENTS

	Page
FOREWORD BY MARIE TURNER, *Superintendent Breathitt County Schools*	V
PREFACE	VII
GENERAL INFORMATION	XIII

PART I. THE GENERAL BACKGROUND

IN THE LAND OF BREATHITT	3
LAND SCULPTURE	10
NATURAL RESOURCES AND ECONOMIC DEVELOPMENT	12
FIRST TRAVELERS	34
FIRST SETTLERS	39
ESTABLISHMENT OF THE COUNTY AND ITS EARLY GOVERNMENT	48
THE EARLY FEUDS OF "BLOODY BREATHITT"	53
JACKSON TODAY	77
THE HISTORY OF JACKSON	84
"BOOK LARNIN'" TO EDUCATION	99
"MEETIN'-HOUSE" TO CHURCH	117

PART II. POINTS OF INTEREST

IN JACKSON AND ENVIRONS	127
IN THE COUNTY	137

PART III. APPENDIX

INDEX	153

ILLUSTRATIONS

FRONTISPIECE   FACING PAGE

MOUNTAIN PATRIARCH 18

SWINGING BRIDGE 26

OXEN AND COAL SLED 34

FARM IN A HOLLOW 42

STIDHAM HOME, JACKSON 50

SHEEP IDYLL 58

BOY WITH A BULL-TONGUE PLOW 66

BEGINNING BRANCH SCHOOL 74

BREATHITT HIGH'S HONOR DRAMATIC GROUP—1939 82

LOST CREEK CONSOLIDATED SCHOOL 90

BREATHITT COUNTY COURTHOUSE 98

JACKSON AROUND 1890 114

JACKSON TODAY 130

GENERAL INFORMATION

Railroads: Louisville and Nashville Railroad (L. & N.)
Bus Lines: Greyhound Lines (Lexington-Hazard run).
Airport: An emergency landing field south of Jackson bordering the L. & N.
Highways: Three state highways—State 15, a hard-surfaced road; State 30, graveled and graded; State 52, unimproved.
Taxis: Fairly regular service to points as far as twenty miles from Jackson for a nominal sum.
Accommodations: One modern hotel in Jackson, and a tourist camp *1.5 m.* south of Jackson; several good restaurants in Jackson.
Amusements and Recreations: Two motion - picture theaters in Jackson; school programs including plays and athletics; fishing in the county's numerous streams, stocked annually by the State; small- and large-mouth bass and wall-eyed pike are the commonest catch; muskellunge and northern pike are found only in the waters of the Middle Fork; hunting is still a popular sport; rabbits, raccoons, opossums and squirrels abound, and red and gray foxes numerous enough to afford fox hunting.
Tourist Information: At the two hotels, Jackson Post Office, and County Courthouse.
Annual Events: Quicksand Harvest Festival at Quicksand, last Thursday and Friday of September; School Fair, third Friday in October.
Population: 1940 Census: Breathitt County (including Jackson), 23,946; Jackson, 2,099.

PART I. THE GENERAL BACKGROUND

IN THE LAND OF BREATHITT

Breathitt (pronounced "Brethit"), land of craggy cone-shaped hills, of streams bearing picturesque names, and of sylvan quiet in ridge-enclosed valleys, has been long and widely famed for the feudal spirit that for three-quarters of a century held over it a bloodstained sway. It has with equal ease achieved national honor and disrepute. Vague happenings steeped in bizarre romanticism have woven around its name a bewitching quality. It is a land where the drab incidents of today are still colored by its medieval past. There is a wild beauty and quaintness in the simple and commonplace things of Breathitt that stimulates the imagination. During World War I the county leaped into the limelight by filling its quota before the draft was imposed. For this reason it was the only county in the United States that did not have to draft a single man into the armed services of the country.

A breed of sturdy men, undaunted by privation and danger, settled in this region, claimed extensive tracts of land and built one- and two-room log cabins. After them their sons and grandsons tilled the soil, sired a numerous progeny, sometimes by two and three wives in succession, drank home-made brandy and corn liquor, often fought in savage disregard of human life, and occasionally stood with bowed heads at the none-too-common "meetin'." They were in the main a rather reckless lot, stubbornly independent, and loyal to a fault. They were illiterate rather than ignorant, more practical than purposeful. They unwittingly preserved much of the quaint speech of their British forbears. A gun and dog were more valuable to them than a sizable tract of land. The half-legendary story of the man who traded an entire "creek of land" containing around three thousand acres for a gun still lives in the memories of many of Breathitt's old-timers. Hunting then as now was considered more worthy of a man and more in keeping with the dignity of his independence than plowing.

For several generations these people were immured in the rugged foothills. There they located their primitive homesteads, and endured for decades the sickening monotony of their isolation. Social life, then as today in more remote sections, largely centered around the most elementary activities of man—funerals, weddings, births. During a large part of the year creekbound communities were and still are marooned by mud and by the unbridged, swollen streams that vein the countryside. In the land of Breathitt there developed a roadless domain based largely on a pinched agricultural existence and on the ways of their fathers and their fathers before them.

Even in their isolation and in their cultural, technological lag the Breathitteers of the nineteenth century were not completely out of touch with the Bluegrass, the growing cities along the Ohio, and even more distant points. In the War between the States contingents of troops from this region traveled beyond the borders of county and State. Prosperous farmers from Breathitt traveled by boat to such commercial centers as Frankfort, Louisville, and Cincinnati, and by land to Mount Sterling, Winchester, and Lexington; while in the earliest period stock was driven to Virginia and New Orleans. County representatives regularly wended their way to Frankfort, the State Capital, where they became familiar with the political questions and practices of the day.

In the chronicles of Breathitt traveling preachers, schoolmasters, and merchants have played important roles. Each of them primarily fulfilled his own particular function, but all of them in common served as links of homespun culture in a homespun frontier society.

The preacher, usually more zealous than learned, helped keep alive the moral consciousness of men who were removed from the elevating influences of more settled, favorably situated communities. Then, too, he relayed news from one community and one family to another and otherwise served as a traveling information bureau. "Meetin's," a name applied only to religious gatherings in the Kentucky mountains, were usually announced months in advance. They drew great concourses from the surrounding countryside. Whole families got up at one or two o'clock in the morning and traveled miles to hear the preaching. It was without question the biggest social event of the year. People who were removed by many creeks and ridges, and as a result seldom saw one another, were drawn together. When "meetin's" were protracted and several preachers held forth, those who had traveled some distance stayed for a few days and then returned home with hopes of attending the next "meetin'" and seeing relatives and friends again.

Many of the teachers came from the Bluegrass and a few even from Virginia. The early schools, housed in windowless log buildings, were haphazard affairs in every respect, yet upon the rudiments of literacy propounded in them were grounded a number of substantial careers. For a period ranging from a few days to three and later five months a meager learning was transmitted down through the decades. It is from such humble beginnings that the modern school system of Breathitt County was evolved.

The thrifty merchant hauling his goods over narrow, rocky roads, overgrown with vegetation and often mud-mired, or up the forks of the Kentucky River on rafts or in flat-bottomed boats was, perhaps, the most appreciated outpost of progress. In the early days, when money was scarce and tobacco was legal tender, the merchant of necessity became a trader. Barter, in which furs and ginseng played a large part, was often the only method of transacting his business. Outside of the sale of timber, coal, and land the principal source of ready cash was infrequent employment on "public works" (any type of common work where a number of men worked for cash) and the sale of "moonshine." Even today many merchants exchange such commodities as lamps, washtubs, soap, and thread for eggs, chickens, a pig, a load of coal, or a pelt.

Not until the era of the railroad in the nineties did Breathitt begin to assume more modern aspects. Changes had been slow and few for over a century, and then the quickening tempo of the machine age disturbed many of the age-old habits of the most remote community. The modernization that took place in the few decades after this surpassed the slow, almost imperceptible, development that had been made during the entire span of its previous history. The natural resources of the county, tapped before the railroad entered, appeared inexhaustible. During the two decades of lush expectations that followed the extension of the railroad to Jackson, the population of the county jumped from 8,705 in 1890 to 14,320 in 1900, and to 17,540 in 1910. At this time the coal and timber interests boomed. A general improvement in homes, stores, schools, and churches took place. The "New Era" was, nevertheless, a period of frontier excesses. The men of courage and foresight who voiced their opposition to the giddy waste of natural resources and the depletion of the land were unheard and unheeded.

A newspaper flourished in the county seat; education was being stressed; and better, quicker mail service was being agitated. The railroad, harbinger of a prosperity that nearly exhausted the natural wealth, remained the symbol of modernism for several decades. It connected an isolated, partly inaccessible region with Lexington and the cities of the Ohio Valley, and brought it into the vast, complex railroad empire then still being laid out. Good roads were still rare luxuries. Travel, as well as the transportation of freight any distance away from the railroad, was a problem and sometimes a tedious and laborious feat dependent on the weather and the vigilance of the county court.

The railroad did not dispel the feud spirit but released it anew by opening up new sources for economic gain. The "B" in Breathitt came to stand for "Bloody." The "killin's" and "shootin's" that took place within the county linked that word inseparably with its name. Yet it was only a resolute few who, taking advantage of the mountaineer's spirit of letting his neighbor alone, inflicted this stigma upon the entire county. The great majority of its people were occupied with the daily tasks of living. Several prominent families at this time competed for the commercial advantages that Jackson then enjoyed as a railroad terminus. They sought to control lumber and coal interests, and in their quest for economic power they resorted to frontier methods. After the railroad had passed beyond Jackson and on through the county, much of the prosperity that it had brought disappeared. It was during this period, however, that the county seat grew from a straggling hamlet into a town of some little commercial importance.

The moneyed families of Breathitt, both of yesterday

and today, laid the foundations of their small fortunes in timber, legal whisky, coal, and land. Sometimes their interests were backed up and strengthened by politics. A few of the early stock drovers and dealers accumulated small fortunes, while some of the large landholders sold their timbered and coal embedded acreage for a comfortable sum. Many of these men left Breathitt with their families and wealth—never to return. A few, particularly during the boom days of Breathitt, opened up commercial houses and thrived during the hectic era of expansion, and then waned when the mountain frontier moved southeastward.

The railroad, coal, timber, prodigal exploitation, and naive optimism characterized the nineteenth century. Centered in Jackson, and shared by landholders in the county, they came to Breathitt late. But the high expectations did not bear fruit—nor were the benefits of the new prosperity ever widespread. The twentieth century came in Breathitt while the ruthless hand of the nineteenth was still scouring its hillsides for marketable timber and gouging in its hillsides for coal.

Visitors or tourists shopping for seventeenth-century quaintness—for the language of Shakespeare and the clan wars of the Scottish Highlands, neither of which exist in the county—will find Breathitt a land where the incrustations of the old are blended with the new. The telephone and the automobile, then later the radio and electricity and, after these, modern trucking facilities have all played a part in refashioning the cultural patter of these so-called "Elizabethan folk." In the speech of its youth, the archaic word, "hit," occasionally slips out along with the latest metropolitan slang. Decided opinions on current events are apt to be encountered in a log cabin whose furnishings and construction may differ little from those of a hundred years ago.

The people of Breathitt are genuine, for they have maintained a high degree of personal integrity. Yet in a business deal they know the art of bargaining. Only their feelings towards outsiders are an open book—to be read and heeded. In other matters emotions are concealed. They are inclined to be wary of the stranger at first, become friendly when they know he means well, but they are hostile when his motives are prying and against their interests. Such an attitude, less noticeable today than in former years, has been built upon the experience of the past when the stranger was usually a "revenooer," or a land agent claiming long-settled land for some corporation. "Out in the county," where the letter as well as the spirit of an older hospitality has been kept alive, it is not unusual to be invited "to *take* a night with us" rather than to "spend" it. Numerous other expressions of hospitality are heard, and many of them are original.

The average Breathitt citizen is wrapped up in politics. If he or one of his blood kin is not running for office, he is lined up as an ardent partisan. During campaigns, especially heated ones, feeling runs high. Liquor and gunfire have played their sad part in primaries and elections. Sharp interparty struggles, sometimes based on old clan feelings, have flared up to tie a few more knots in the tangle of Breathitt's highly personalized politics.

A hard-surfaced highway (State 15) threads its way through the center of the county from north to south connecting Winchester and the Bluegrass with Jackson, Hazard, Whitesburg, and the Virginia line at Pound Gap. A graveled road (State 30) links Jackson with Paintsville, Salyersville on the northeast, and Booneville on the west, and another (State 52) leads more directly west from Jackson to Beattyville in Lee County and then on to Richmond in Madison County.

A wider diffusion of public education in the county, together with opportunities in numerous mountain schools throughout the Appalachians, have helped bridge the cultural gap of a century and a half. Two modern public high schools, a junior college, several consolidated schools of up-to-date construction, and school busses represent recent trends that are in step with tomorrow. Jackson, a peaceful county seat with an air of modernity in keeping with its size, may be disturbing.

In spite of the fact that Breathitt County has been classified as the "most non-industrial, non-agricultural, yet super-rural county in the United States," its people have remained virile and fertile; they have not been physically broken by the poverty of their soil and other resources. Breathitt families almost invariably come large. Hidden in its coves like unpolished gems are many of its sons and daughters who possess striking natural beauty, a quick sense of humor, mental alertness, and all the other qualities that endow them with true and genuine nobility.

This is, then, the saga of pioneering, of mountain homesteaders, and a long-persisting frontier in the land of Breathitt; it depicts a people who today are rich in personality and woefully poor in material possessions.

This is the land of Breathitt!

LAND SCULPTURE

Breathitt, spread out over nearly five hundred square miles of hills, hollows, and bottom lands in east central Kentucky, lies near the northwestern rim of the mountain coal field. The county is located entirely in the upper Kentucky basin, and is drained by the North and Middle forks of this river and their numerous tributaries of which Troublesome and Quicksand creeks are the most important. It is part of a comparatively youthful uplift that arose eons ago out of a warm, murky sea. Since then it has been worn down and cut through by innumerable streams; the forms and features of its landscape fashioned by all the weathering hands of nature. Ridges, cone-shaped hills, and winding gorges give it the rugged character that only attain more dramatic proportions in the heart of the Appalachians to the southeast. In Breathitt the rock-bestrewn foothills are occasionally emboldened near their crests by turreted or pedestal rocks and by cliffs. In the Spring Fork and Upper Quicksand sections there are many cliffs which, like those seen along the highway in Wolfe County, stand out sheerly against the skyline like ancient castellations. Rock houses have in many places been sculptured out of sandstone outcroppings by wind, rain, and frost. In a few places streams have gouged their way through rock-bound, closely pressed hills, and at numerous points in the county the two forks of the Kentucky River flow beneath rocky precipices.

Several of these fascinating, oddly shaped features of Breathitt's land sculpture are found in and around Jackson. On the hill known as Highknob a flat-topped pedestal rock with naturally formed pigeonholes adjoins a sheltering half-mushroom formation. On both sides of the Panhandle, at the point where it begins to broaden into the Panbowl and massive rocks stairstep half way to the peak, rock houses, one of them with pigeonholes, have been cut out by erosive forces.

Although its elevations are not of great prominence, Breathitt belongs to the Kentucky mountain country. In the Kentucky River bottoms, along the Lee and Wolfe County lines in the western part of the county, the altitude is as low as 690 feet, and at the mouth of Quicksand Creek, as well as at other confluences in the county, elevations are much lower than those of the Bluegrass towns. Jackson, the county seat, has an altitude 157 feet lower than Lexington. Elkbutt Knob, at the head of Troublesome's Caney on the Perry-Breathitt County line, has an altitude of over 1,650 feet and is therefore the highest elevation in the county. On the tops of several of the highest mountains, entirely within the county, elevations reach 1,530 feet. North of Jackson, State Highway 15 winds to the top of Frozen Mountain which has an altitude of 1,500 feet at this point. Highknob, a tree-crested cone overlooking Jackson on the southwest, is one of the high points in Breathitt. In the north central section, including Wilhurst and Stevenson, the elevations are around 1,000 feet, while in the southernmost part, around Wolf Coal, they are around 1,300 feet.

Elevations, land shapes, and rocky outcrops present in their variety a fairly uniform pattern throughout the county. Only in the northeast, near the Magoffin and Wolfe County lines, and in the west along the Lee and Owsley County lines, are its hills noticeably less rugged than in other parts. Here the land is not so rocky and is more sloping. Since the sandstones that underlay the surface are not too resistant to erosion, there are a series of fairly broad valleys along the main streams. Near the headwaters of the smaller streams the hills are steeper, squeezed closer together, and there is little level land. The narrow V-shaped valleys that characterize most of the mountain sections are found here and along the smaller creeks and their branches. Along the North and Middle forks and along their larger tributaries such as Troublesome, Quicksand, Frozen, Cane, and Old Buck, bottom lands in some places extend in wide, rich acreage to foothills some distance from the stream. At other points a narrow strip, sometimes sloping and at other times moderately level, serves as tables upon which the fertile soils of the hillside are washed.

NATURAL RESOURCES AND ECONOMIC DEVELOPMENT

When the first settlers came into the Breathitt area they found a land abounding in varied natural wealth. Surface coal had already been noted by Christopher Gist as early as 1750. Magnificent, breath-taking forests covered its hills and bottom lands; streams were alive with fish; game roamed the tangled wilderness; and the soil of the bottoms was stored with the fertility of ages. Embedded under the surface, and untapped until more modern times, were deposits of natural gas and, in very small quantities, oil.

The tempo of exploiting these natural resources was slow for almost a century. Bottom lands were taken up by the first settlers who were sturdy homesteaders. Later, as the population increased, the headwater hills were peopled and steep hillsides brought under cultivation. Timber was cut and coal was mined on a comparatively small scale early in the history of this section, but not until the era of the railroad did wholesale exploitation take place.

Farming and Agriculture "Side Lines"

Although Breathitt is almost totally dependent on farming for a livelihood, it has been described, with exaggeration, as "the most non-industrial, non-agricultural, yet super-rural county in the United States." The agricultural picture of this mountain county naturally bears little relationship to its land area of 309,120 acres (483 square miles). While a little more than two-thirds (235,693 acres) of this was in farms in 1934, an average farm year, less than a third (99,885 acres) was classified as crop land which includes plowable pasture. Bottoms, some of them quite broad and long, are the only fertile strips of land. The two best farming sections are in Frozen Valley in the northern part of the county, badly flooded in 1939, and along the Middle Fork in the southwestern quarter.

Three-fourths (72.2 per cent) of all those gainfully employed in Breathitt, when the 1930 census was taken, were engaged in agriculture. That it was on a subsistence level is indicated by the fact that only 51 farms reported an average value of farm products in excess of $700 per farm. These were farms that produced livestock and dairy products. The per capita value of farm products in this census was $68.84 and the net value of all farm products was $1,212,182. The county's 3,590 farms were valued at $2,518,673. The average Breathitt farm was 65.7 acres, valued at $702, or $10.69 per acre. Operation of these farms was divided between 1,981 full owners, 191 part owners, 1,250 by cash-rent tenants, 167 by sharecroppers, and 1 by a manager.

Over 98 per cent of all farm land in Breathitt County was under the agricultural soil conservation program of the Federal Government in 1938. Acreage under this program included almost 22,000 in corn which, despite its notable decrease from 36,771 in 1934, is still the principal crop. The ever present cornfield, many of them flung crazily across the brows of steep hillsides, are the most familiar sight of the countryside. There were also 10 acres in wheat, 290 in oats, 170 in sorghum and 1,800 in vegetables. Acreage used for non-depleting purposes included about 40,000 for pasturage and over 7,000 in cover crops. The total crop acreage under the soil program was 24,683, while the total acreage was 87,358. Under this program, denuded hills are being sown in clover, and seedlings have been planted in many sections.

Tobacco has become an increasingly important cash crop in certain sections of the county. About 400 acres gave it fourth place among farm crops in 1939. In 1934, 203 acres produced 104,061 pounds of tobacco. Other leading farm crops in 1934 were Irish potatoes, sweet potatoes, hay, and sorghum. Sheep, which are suited to the county's hills, are again coming back, and hogs and cattle have increased greatly in the past decade. In 1934 there were 8,594 cattle, of which 5,321 were cows and heifers over two years old, 9,788 hogs, and 1,174 sheep. Work animals at this time numbered 788 horses and 2,280 mules.

Agriculturally, Breathitt County has undergone

many changes. The agricultural statistics of the 1840 United States census pictured a county of diversified crops, livestock, and home industries. Although the margin of error is undoubtedly great, especially in the remote mountainous Breathitt of 1840, it is evident that the agricultural wealth per capita was much greater then than in more recent decades. Breathitt, of course, was considerably larger in area at that time.

Indian corn, the principal crop of the first settlers, was the foundation of the county's agricultural economy. The bread used then was corn bread. In well-to-do families a little wheat was sometimes grown and flour kept for company or special occasions. The number of bushels of the various grains grown in 1839 were: Indian corn, 91,-185; oats, 7,749; wheat, 1,628; rye, 522; buckwheat, 12.

Meat at first was wild game, but many years before 1840 the hog had taken first place and has held it ever since. There were then almost four hogs for every single individual in the county (swine, 9,674), neat cattle numbered 3,517 head, or around one and one-half head of beef for each individual. There was one and a fraction horse or mule for every three people, which meant an average of two or more of these work animals for each family (758 horses and mules), and there was a little over one sheep for every person (sheep, 2,294.). Poultry of all kinds was valued at $842. Chickens, brought in at the beginning, have never received the attention they deserve as a meat and for their eggs.

Tobacco, interestingly enough, was grown at this time; 2,648 pounds being gathered in 1839. Cotton, which is not grown at all today in Breathitt, was raised to the extent of 4,270 pounds. This was mainly used to make mattresses, quilts, and other home articles. The number of bushels of potatoes grown was 2,894, or a little over one bushel for each individual. Potatoes and sweet potatoes were next in importance to corn as a food, then beans, and peas, and the other garden vegetables. In early times turnips were an important crop.

Other crops included hay (73 tons), and hemp and flax (three tons). Wool ranked second to cotton in textiles, with 3,584 pounds clipped in 1839. The number of pounds of soap made was 21,764; of tallow candles, 1,218;

of beeswax manufactured, 312; of sugar made, 12,377. The value of home-made, or family goods, was placed at $7,024.

Orchards were set out at the time settlements were made. In this connection it is interesting to note that the first site of the county seat at Quicksand was staked out in an orchard which was then referred to as "old." Fruits, together with vegetables, were dried for winter use. When potters were able to supply jars and jugs, they were pressed into use for jams and juices, and the preservation of dried fruits and vegetables. Milk, usually sour, or buttermilk, was the chief drink at mealtime; little cheese was made. Tea and coffee were unknown during the early period. Hominy, which is still made by many mountain people, was an important staple in the diet of the early and later settlers.

Livestock was fed on mast and the lush herbage for many decades after the first settlements were made. Most of the early livestock farmers fed their cattle and hogs on peavine and similar herbage in the summer, and on cane and other forage in the winter. As long as soft, edible nuts, and rich, wild forage lasted, stock raising was a fairly profitable enterprise.

An agricultural side line that helped round out the farming economy of Breathitt and has brought ready cash into the county was ginseng gathering. The ginseng root has been shipped for around two centuries from this country to China where it is considered a cure-all. Modern medical science has now debunked the many claims made for it. In Breathitt, the gathering of wild "sang" has been more important, commercially, than its cultivation. "Senging," as it was called, was an important source of income during the early days. Sometimes a whole family, but usually women and boys, would go into the hills at dawn with hoes and sacks. At the end of the day they would lug home their sackful of ginseng root which they later exchanged at the nearest general store for staples and textiles, and sometimes for cash. Many years ago the sale of ginseng in summer and coonskins in winter was about the only way many boys had of obtaining pocket money. Sometimes women of the middle period of the county's history also dug yellowroot (golden seal), snakeroot, and bloodroot, which were then marketable.

Ginseng brought fancy prices for many years. A

woodland full of ginseng was always a backlog that could be turned into cash. Within the memory of Mr. Tom Haddix, of Haddix, the root brought $7.00 a pound. The World War caused a slump in the ginseng market. In July, 1914, ginseng sold in Louisville for $6.50 a pound. For a long time after the war started no shipments were sent to China, and the price declined.

Bee swarms have been captured and their woodland hives robbed from the earliest times. This was an important source of food for many of the early settlers. Only an occasional farmer, however, attempted the culture of bees for the marketing of honey. Old-fashioned bee gums, many still dotting the hillsides of Breathitt, are made from the trunks of large trees. Lengths, two and one-half feet, were hollowed and dressed inside. Sticks were then placed in them to form cells for the bees to store their honey. James Noble, the son of Nathan, is remembered as a great bee man. At one time he had over a hundred stands of bees. Some of the natural gums he found, usually a hollow sycamore, held as much as twenty bushels. He strained the honey, put it in barrels, and it was boated to Beattyville. One of his barrels, which had been bought from him for $30, sold for $60 down the river. Honey was locally sold for $1.00 a gallon.

The making of sugar from the sap of sugar maple trees, as indicated in the 1840 census, was an important home industry. A farmer who, towards the end of the nineteenth century, made a name for himself in the manufacture of this sugar was S. E. Taulbee, of the Frozen Creek section. His orchard, consisting of about 75 trees, was located in a bottom and extended up the hillside. The trees were tapped in March and usually in the morning after the sun had shone on the trees several hours. The sap was run off into wooden troughs about three feet long and six inches deep. Larger troughs, holding about 30 gallons, were used to hold larger quantities of sap. Three cast-iron kettles containing 12, 15, and 20 gallons were used by Mr. Taulbee to boil the sap down. It would usually take a day and half of the night to boil it down to the point where it would be ready for a "stir-off" the following day. About two hours were then required to boil the syrup to the sugar point. When this was done, it was poured into teacups, and when they ran out small bowls were used. The teacup size sold for ten cents each or eleven for $1.00, and the maple sugar was marketed through Hargis Brothers, Jackson.

The history of agricultural development in Breathitt, as in most sections of the country, is one of soil depletion, erosion, and inefficient farming methods. But, unlike many other sections, the land available for crops and pasturage is limited by its topography while its agricultural economy, even under the best conditions, will be severely overtaxed by a relatively large population. Agriculturally, Breathitt has a Spartan future. Today, Breathitt farming is below the subsistence level. Hogs, sheep, and milk cows are best suited to the farming of the county as cash farm products and are being encouraged for this reason by the county agricultural agent.

The present program is necessarily one of conservation and agricultural education. Approximately 600 boys and girls belong to 4-H clubs in 22 communities, while 51 students belong to the county high school's Future Farmers of America Club. The county high school also has an agricultural department which bases its courses on the practical needs of Breathitt County. In a better understanding of land usage and a more varied program, there is promise of better agricultural conditions.

The Rise and Fall of Coal Production

In coal mining as in agriculture, Breathitt has seen better days. Coal and natural gas, the principal mineral resources of the county, are the only ones of any commercial importance. There are about seven coal seams of which only three, (1) fireclay or No. 4, (2) Whitesburg or No. 3, and (3) flag or No. 7, can be profitably worked. The upper veins of coal have been depleted, and lower unworked veins can be mined only by shafting to their level. The R. T. Davis mine, near Jackson, is the only large mine now operating in the county. Elsewhere individual farmers, sometimes with a helper or two, work "coal diggings" for a local market and for their home.

At one time Breathitt ranked high in coal production, but in 1934 it slipped down into nineteenth place among the State's twenty-two coal producing counties. Annual coal production has fluctuated widely over the last few decades. In 1904, 42,355 tons were mined and in 1913, 6,000 tons. During the World War and later during the "boom" of the 1920's production followed the upward surge of the heavy industries. In 1925 the county produced 177,029 tons of coal, and in 1929 coal production reached 208,656 tons. By 1934 it had fallen to 71,401 tons, a decrease of 64.4 per cent during 1928-34. There were 308 employed coal miners in the county in 1928, but in 1934 this had fallen to 194. During this same period the average number of days worked fell from 229 to 140.

Small amounts of coal to supply the needs of the primitive mountain home have undoubtedly been "stripped" since the first settlements. Wood, as long as it was plentiful, was used almost without exception for fuel. Coal production for a market "down the river" was already well established on the Kentucky River in 1835 when 75,000 bushels (3,000 tons), valued at $9,000, were marketed. The Board of Internal Improvement reported for 1835-36 that the principal veins mined at that time did not effectually supply their Lexington and Frankfort markets. Mines referred to in the report were near the mouth of the South Fork, near the mouth of Troublesome Creek, sixty miles up the North Fork, "where it is found in better quality than in any part of the United States"; and near Hazard. Among the mines reported on the main river the following year were twelve or fourteen on the North Fork between the Middle Fork and Hazard, and several on Troublesome and Quicksand creeks. The Troublesome mines were located near its mouth and up its north fork, where coal from openings on George's Creek was highly valued in central Kentucky. The mines on Quicksand were located from one to four miles above its mouth. The "Round Bottom" coal, mined on Quicksand, carried at base a superior cannel, averaging about two feet in thickness.

The Haddix mines at the mouth of Troublesome Creek were probably worked as extensively in 1838 as any other mines in the upper Kentucky River basin. The cannel coal, 273 feet above low water, which was mined here was noted for its hard and brittle qualities. It sold at a higher price because it was more expensive to mine than other coals and because it was considered a better coal. Cannel coal can be split very thin with an ax and the thin pieces will catch fire from a lighted match.

MOUNTAIN PATRIARCH

Shipments of coal down the Kentucky River in 1838 totaled 200,000 bushels or 8,000 tons. In the census of 1840 Clay County was credited with a production of 88,950 bushels, Estill (including Lee) with 98,525 bushels, and Breathitt with 21,017 bushels. There were twenty-eight men employed as miners at this time in the county and the capital invested was placed at $442. The census of 1860 mentions only Breathitt County, where there were six establishments and a product valued at $7,550. In 1880, 500 tons were taken from a mine on Spicer's Branch (North Fork).

In 1854-55 the Kentucky Geological Survey noted that, "The main coal has been entered in several places near the river above and below Jackson and an extensive business is here carried on in the coal trade which supplies most of the ready cash circulating in the country." Mines for commercial production were opened on streams capable of floating a flatboat or a raft, at least during "high tide." Practically all the mining and shipping of coal was done by the land-owning farmers, principally in the autumn and winter when they were not engaged in lumbering or tilling the soil.

Mr. Tom Haddix, whose father, William G., owned coal mines at Haddix, remembers trips to Frankfort and other points en route in coal boats and on log rafts. Coal was mined then with a hand pick, dirt being removed with a mattock, a grubbing hoe, and shovel. When rock was struck, it was removed with a two-pointed pick. In a cannel coal mine the common coal lies on top of the vein, and is about one foot thick. This was cut away before the cannel coal could be reached. At one place near Haddix a hill was mined through from one side to the other, or about 600 feet from opening to opening. Mr. Tom Haddix helped get out what was considered the largest block of cannel coal ever mined in those days, and one of the largest blocks ever to leave the Kentucky River Basin, a four-foot cube. A Scotchman came here, looked at the cannel coal, and then ordered a block to take to the World's Fair at Chicago in the 1890's. It was cut out with a hand pick, and pulled out of the mine with a yoke of oxen. The Scotchman paid $10 for this block which took a premium at the World's Fair. Afterwards it was called "Premium" coal. The mines at Haddix, first opened around 1852, were shut down in 1928.

Until the entry of the railroad, coal production was comparatively small in Breathitt County. Mines were centered around Jackson, on the North Fork below the town, and near the mouths of Troublesome and Quicksand creeks. After the Kentucky Union Railroad reached Jackson, in 1891, practically the same mines were worked and few changes were made in mining methods. Shortly before the entrance of the railroad, small companies were formed, fairly extensive tracts of coal lands were leased or purchased, and more men were employed in each mine. Coal was shipped by rail only from Lee and Breathitt of the upper Kentucky River counties. In 1903 a line was extended from Jackson up Frozen Creek into Wolfe County, and a high grade cannel coal was mined at a number of openings along this road. It was not until 1913, when the railroad was laid into Letcher County, that this region became important for its coal production.

Articles in *The Jackson Hustler* "drummed" the potentialities of the county when the railroad entered as vigorously as a boom town chamber of commerce. In the issue of June 21, 1889, land speculators were reported as paying $2.00 to $200 per acre for coal and timber lands:

> The Progress of mineral developments in this section of the mountains is still unabated. New veins and banks of coal are being discovered almost every day. In fact, our people as a class, are just now beginning to see the necessity of having all their banks opened so that the coal may be seen. They have learned by time and experience that a speculator is ten times more apt to make purchase when he can see what he is buying than he is where he has to act by heresay or guess work. . . .

In an article entitled "Wealth Untold," *The Hustler* of March 20, 1891, exaggeratedly reported thirty-two feet of coal in six veins on the same piece of land. After mixing a little imagination with a little addition, it concluded that "These things seem fabulous, but they show for themselves. Surely we have a great country, awaiting the touch of capital and enterprise to develop its wealth."

The touch of capital and enterprise was somewhat like the golden touch of Midas. It was a blessing with a boomerang.

Timber, Logging and Sawmills

None of the fine virgin forests that once covered the hills of Breathitt have been spared. The stately hardwoods that gave the land a richness and splendor of scenery, conserved its soil and provided a reserve of natural wealth, have been replaced by second growth and in some sections even third growth timber that is thin and scrawny.

Logging was already an important cash side line of the hill farmer when the county was created. Logs were rafted down the river and sold for "coin of the realm," or else exchanged directly for articles to be taken back home. In the 1835-36 *State Senate Journal* there is mention of 3,000 logs being floated down the Kentucky from the vicinity of the Three Forks, and in 1838 (*House Journal*) there was an estimated annual shipment of 1,000 logs down the Middle Fork.

Cutting was not extensive, however, until the 1890's. Poplar and walnut were the only timbers that had been noticeably cut before this time. *The Hustler* carried a notice in the issue of April 3, 1891, that between two and three million feet of walnut lumber, cut in Letcher County, passed down the river on a recent tide. It belonged to the Singer Sewing Machine Company and was on its way to Madison, Indiana. Another item in the same issue of the Jackson newspaper reported that "During the great freshet, February, 1890, a great deal of walnut lodged along the river from a lumber raft that got loose on the upper Kentucky. Last Thursday a boat passed down, picking it up. . . ."

Allen Moore and his son Daniel are in many respects representative of the timbermen who operated in the county before outside or "foreign" capital came in. They took up a large tract of timberland near the Breathitt-Perry line after the War between the States and engaged in a big logging business. Logs were hauled to the creeks during high water, or before heavy rains set in. They floated down to the confluence of Bush's Creek with the North Fork and then were rafted to Beattyville and Frankfort where they were sold. Often the owner and some of his employees made their home on the raft of floating logs during these trips, cooking their provisions and eating corn pones made at home before leaving. After selling the logs at Frankfort or some other market, they purchased needed supplies and usually some trinket for the members of their families, and then set out on the forest trails back to their homes. Allen Moore and his son Daniel also owned a water-driven saw- and gristmill which operated until the death of Daniel in 1892. During the great flood of 1893 the dam broke and this mill was washed away.

Sawmilling, however, did not become an important or profitable business until the end of the nineteenth century. The sawmill reported in the 1840 census, and numerous others that were built for a half century afterwards, principally supplied local needs. There was an old saying in the mountains that "if you want revenge, give your enemy a sawmill." This proverb passed out during the last decade of the century.

Around 1894 Jackson's railroad-inspired boom was strengthened with the establishment of three new mills in the town. Wagons hauling lumber to the depot for shipment were part of the daily scene. Staves and crossties were taken from the river and loaded on railroad cars for shipment.

Chris Anderson, born on the Middle Fork in Breathitt County, logged on the Kentucky River many years. In the retirement of his Pine Mountain cabin in Letcher County he recalled his logging days in an interview with Rene Niles, feature writer for the Louisville *Courier-Journal* ("Pine Mountain Yarning Logger," Sunday Magazine Section, Nov. 26, 1939):

> ... We took out mostly poplar logs—four, five, six feet through: they were big logs! We'd git six or eight oxen to snake them logs outa the places where they fell and roll 'em into a little valley-like, where the spring rains would bring a freshet. And we'd make the kinda dam we call a splash-dam. Hit was made of small logs, leaned outward at the edge, with more logs underneath. And when the rains came, they'd collect back of our splash-dam. Now we'd build a gate at the rim of the dam, and when all them logs would git to floatin' around, we'd pull out the gate and the water would come like a cloudburst and the logs come with it. Often as not, the logs would seem like they was ahead of the water, but I reckon we weren't a-lookin' straight. If the logs didn't get over to the river, we would have to build another splash-dam and do it all over again. Once we got our logs in the river, we headed 'em into the lumber company's boom, and the lumber company would buy 'em. We marked 'em by branding 'em on the end, but mean fellers would come along and saw the end off our logs sometimes and put their

own brand on instead. This would happen quite a few times to some logs, till they got down to stovewood size for bein' sawed over and over. Sometimes hit was the lumber companies that robbed us. I recollect how my father logged down $1,000 worth or maybe $1,200 worth of walnut logs. They was big ones and beauties, but when the lumber company got done with the old man, he got about $125 for his lumber. The old man was none too glad over it—I mean he didn't go out and get eight couples and a fiddler and run a set of steps. . . . I never did any raftin' of logs. Hit was a dangerous business; men got all ground up when them rafts turned over. And then sometimes the rafts would sink and the men went down with 'em. Why, I hear tell that they be some poplar logs in the Kentucky River yet. . . .

The log stealing mentioned by Chris Anderson often assumed serious proportions. *The Hustler* of April 17, 1891, commented: "In some places on the river this stealing is going on to such extent and is so tolerated and encouraged by people regarded as respectable that it is almost impossible to arrest or convict those engaged in this nefarious business." Sometimes these sawed-off logs were taken up the smaller creeks and manufactured into shingles and other lumber products. One of the most familiar advertisements in *The Jackson Hustler* in 1891 was a warning to log thieves.

A "log-run," which occurred when the rivers rose, was the climax of the logging season. Thousands of logs, many of them carried out of headwaters, raced down the river. Gangs of men worked at the various booms along the river; sometimes one would lose his life. Spiked poles were used to bring branded logs into the boom where they properly belonged, while other logs floated by. As the men worked on into the night, pine torches and fires of cannel coal lit up the booms. At times the high water was solidly covered from bank to bank and as far up and down the river as one could see. During the 1900's and 1910's telephones were installed by the various concerns along the river, and information on the stage of the river and the approximate number of logs floating by per minute was rapidly relayed from one point to the next. A typical run was reported in the Louisville *Courier-Journal* on March 10, 1915:

> The Kentucky River at Beattyville shows a twenty-foot rise and logs are rushing by the thousands, but are being caught in the booms.
> The Day booms [at Jackson] are holding splendidly and all this

company needs is more men. These they are offering every inducement to obtain. The people are responding heartily, and even preachers, lawyers, bankers, and prominent business men are at work on the booms catching logs. Ten thousand logs had already been caught at eight o'clock to-night. The rain continues to pour and the river is still rising.

An immense quantity of logs piled for miles in Quicksand Fork of Kentucky River, broke up just at dark to-night and at ten o'clock to-night are passing Jackson at the rate of 15,000 per hour. The logs are running so fast that only a small percent of them can run into the booms. The logs are also running thicker in the main river and this run will be longer continued and more steady than the Quicksand run.

Several days of rain here [Jackson] and in the mountains at the head of the river has resulted in a twelve-foot rise in the North Fork. Telephone messages from Hazard and other points farther up the river indicate that practically all the logs have been splashed out of the creeks, Big Leatherwood alone contributing its quota of 15,000 logs. Logs began to reach here to-day and the number continues to increase. . . . Many of the logs are permitted to pass, but about half are caught in the Swann-Day Company's boom. The booms are in good condition and easily hold 25,000 logs. This company's boom at Beattyville will hold 30,000 logs. All logs which are permitted to pass this point will be caught at Beattyville. A large number of men will work at the booms here all night. It is not expected that the biggest run of logs will be here before midnight.

The last of the large lumber companies, Mowbray and Robinson at Quicksand, left Breathitt County in 1925, after a decade or so of continuous operation. Much of their timber was cleared from the immense holding of the Kentucky Union Land Company. Mowbray and Robinson also purchased tracts of valuable timber which was hauled to their mill at Quicksand on a narrow-gauge railroad laid down to the scene of their cuttings. The Eastern Kentucky Hardwood Company, probably the most extensive timber enterprise during the history of Breathitt County, owned five mills near the mouth of Quicksand Creek before this. Another important mill was operated at Jackson by the Day Brothers Lumber Company, and later as the Swann-Day Company was one of the largest sawmills in this region.

At the present time (1940) the only milling concern in Breathitt County is a stave company about a mile east of Quicksand on State 30. The mill is a portable outfit that makes white oak staves for whisky barrels and also tobacco poles. It has been located in the vicinity of Quicksand since 1936, employing about a dozen men.

Early Salt Works

A small industry that filled one of the needs of an isolated society was the manufacture of salt. It was carried on for a longer period in the Kentucky basin than in other sections of the State, and it did not die out in Breathitt until the railroad reached Jackson. An early center of salt making in eastern Kentucky was near Manchester in Clay County.

In commenting on the difference in prices around 1840 and those in the second decade of the twentieth century, J. Green Trimble mentioned "Robert F. Brashears, who lived on the river at the mouth of Leatherwood, owned salt works, and furnished us a boatload of salt, which we sold at $1.75 a bushel, or $10.50 for a barrel of seven bushels." This salt works was established in the early 1830's on Leatherwood Creek in Perry County, 113 miles from Beattyville, by General White and Colonel Brashear, and for a time produced 250 bushels a week, which was considered sufficient for local needs. In 1838, as noted in the *Kentucky House Journal*, they had a capacity of fifty bushels a day and water enough for three times that amount. The *House Journal* of 1818 mentions that salt was manufactured "high up" on the Middle Fork, and an act of 1821 refers to the Garrard Salt Works, probably located at the confluence of the Middle Fork and Cutshin Creek in Leslie County.

One of the more important salt works in eastern Kentucky was located on Troublesome Creek about one and one-half miles upstream from the mouth of Lost Creek. In 1838 a report to the Kentucky House of Representatives stated that this works had a daily capacity of ten bushels. This is undoubtedly the Breathitt Salt Works referred to in the 1840 U. S. Census as having a product of seventy bushels and with three employees.

This early salt works was near present-day Haddix, a hamlet about eight miles from Jackson, on the site of the L. & N. depot. In 1837 William Haddix and his son-in-law, Col. Louis C. Bohanon, drilled 420 feet for the well. At two hundred they struck a vein of coal variously reported from eleven to sixteen feet thick. They drilled on through it until they reached briny water. This water was first piped into a cistern and then it was run into salt kettles, which were placed over a hot, stone furnace fire. After the water boiled down, the salt was put up by the bushel. Mr. Tom Haddix, of Haddix, whose father was co-founder of this salt works, still has in his possession a small salt kettle with a capacity of thirty gallons. Most of the kettles were larger. The brine obtained at this well produced a bushel of salt from 100 gallons. The water obtained at the Leatherwood Salt Works yielded a bushel from sixty-five to seventy gallons when economically worked.

Salt was sold to people of the surrounding county at $1.00 per bushel and the surplus was shipped down the Kentucky River as far as Irvine, Estill County, in large canoes. It was sold along the way and, when the supply was gone, the canoes returned. At one time this salt works could turn out 100 bushels a day.

Another old salt works in the vicinity was at the end of the present Lost Creek Bridge. Around 1875 salt was $2.00 a bushel, although the price was regularly $1.00 until the railroad reached Jackson. People bought this salt as fast as it was made. In an earlier period, when many settlers were still coming in, they had to go to Clay County for salt. Salt works, near present-day Copeland Station at the mouth of Shoal Branch, were operated and closed before the War between the States. A salt well was also owned by the Noble family. All of these wells had to be bored through a vein of coal about two hundred feet down.

Gas, Oil, and Sandstone

The surface rocks of Breathitt consist of an alternating series of sandstones, shales, and coals, all of which are of Pottsville (lower Pennsylvania) age. Bedded rocks in the northwestern part of the county normally dip to the southeast, but elsewhere dips are local in response to the influence of the great downward thrust of the earth in eastern Kentucky—a flexure which loops through southeastern Breathitt and bisects the county.

Natural gas has been developed on the waters of Frozen Creek in the northern part of the county, and at several points along the North and Middle forks. Deposits were tapped near Jackson in 1936 to give the town

SWINGING BRIDGE

gas for heating and cooking purposes. Petroleum has been commercially produced in small quantities from the coniferous sand in the northwestern part of Breathitt, near the Wolfe County line. Only a few wells have been drilled and, since their flow was small, they have been sealed.

Sandstone suitable for buildings, bridge abutments, and road packing occurs abundantly and has been quarried in various parts of the county. The new Breathitt County Jail and the main building of Highland Institute have been built of native sandstone. Alluvial sand and gravel suitable for cement and concrete construction are found in the bed of the North and Middle forks of the Kentucky River. The last geological structural oil and gas map of Breathitt County was issued in 1927.

Travel and Transportation

The meager and belated development of the natural resources of the upper Kentucky River Basin during the nineteenth century was caused by slow, hazardous means of transportation. Even today modern transportation facilities do not reach remote sections where the automobile has to be abandoned for the mule during all or the greater part of the year. For many decades some of the more populous communities of this region could not be reached by dependable roads—for there were none. Local distances of 40, 50, and as high as 100 miles were traveled by "shank's mare," and on horse- or muleback. Forty miles was considered a short day's walk. During the earlier days men and boys sometimes walked to such distant points as Prestonsburg, Irvine, and Mount Sterling with pelts and other light articles for sale. The North Fork of the Kentucky River, the principal means of freighting products in and out of this section of the Highlands, was at best uncertain and completely out of the question during certain times of the year.

The traditions of some of the pioneer families of Breathitt relate that their forbears made part of their way into this region in canoes. Mr. Henry Gay, who came from Virginia in the 1800's, brought with him a canoe which he carried on his shoulders when crossing from one stream to another. He came down the North Fork and settled on a stream (Gay's Creek) later named for him.

It is said that often while floating along the streams in the wilderness he had to use his paddle to part the canes that grew so tall and thick that they met overhead. Other settlers walked in, while more fortunate ones had pack horses or mules on which the women and smaller children sometimes rode. In driving stock to the Virginia and Bluegrass markets the drovers walked both ways.

Until the State Legislature appropriated money to improve the North Fork, river transportation was made with heavy odds against the cargo and navigator. Even after improvements were made, rafting and boating on the narrow upper Kentucky was about as uncertain as a lone poker chip in the hand of a greenhorn. The channel from mouth to headwaters was blocked with islands, sand and gravel bars, "narrers," and other obstructions. Vine-entwined trees formed low, leafy ceilings at many places along the sinuous stream. The most threatening obstructions were the roughs and narrows of rocky gorges. Here, in short and frequent bends, easily eroded shale had accumulated, leaving high reefs in the channel. On the North Fork narrows extended from Beattyville to the mouth of Holly Creek, a distance of about twenty-five miles. Soon after the lands along the river valleys were taken up, man-made obstructions—timber booms and mill and fish dams—added to the difficulties of navigation.

In spite of all these hazards, transportation by water began at an early date. The river was navigable, however, only during certain months of the year when there was sufficient volume to cover these obstructions. Mountain merchants floated out their products at tide, as they call high or floodwater, in sturdily built push-boats.

Push-boats were nothing more than barges. They were primitively built on three yellow poplar logs, some thirty inches in diameter. The bottom was laid on these logs and a false bottom four or five inches from the real bottom protected the cargo from damage through leakage. The boat was boarded on all four sides and curved from the bottom on both ends like sled runners. The larger barges were around sixty feet long eight wide and three feet deep. Merchandise weighing from ten to thirty thousand pounds, depending on the size and condition of the boat, was sometimes piled to a height of ten feet. From three to seven men operated the boat. Knobbed poles were used to push the boat against the current. In the earlier days, grapevines, some as thick as a man's arm, were used as cables to tie boats and rafts to trees and rocks. A trip upstream from Jackson to Hazard took around three weeks or a month.

Before the road from Jackson to the mouth of War Creek was made, around 1840, all the freight for the county had to be brought in boats from Clay's Ferry, about eighty-five miles down the river. "'The merchants and business men . . . had much trouble in getting their freight by the river during the summer season . . . They frequently had to employ ox teams to pull the boats through the shoals when the water was low."—[J. GREEN TRIMBLE, *Recollections*, p. 18.]

In 1834 Col. John Haddix put his horse, Printer, on a Frankfort-bound coal boat at the mouth of Troublesome in order to ride him back home. The horse went through all right, but when he was taken from the boat he couldn't stand up. After a short rest, he carried the colonel home.

The North Fork was declared navigable by the State Legislature in 1821 from its mouth to Line Fork, which enters the stream just above the salt wells at the mouth of Leatherwood. In 1835 improvements were begun on the upper river to supplement canalization of the main river. During the following decade innumerable artificial obstructions were removed and over $8,000 was spent. These improvements were made mostly to benefit the salt, coal, and timber industries which were attaining commercial importance. Between 1837 and 1841, approximately $3,500 was spent on the North Fork, a sum somewhat larger than that spent on the South Fork.

Later improvements along the North Fork were made solely to help the coal industry. Around this time the State Board of Internal Improvement reported that the North Fork could be made navigable for steamboats of eighty tons burden as far as Troublesome Creek at a cost of $9,140 per mile for a distance of fifty-five miles. This was never done, and Beattyville remained the head of navigation as far as steamboats were concerned, and the port of upper river commerce. An expenditure of $5,000 was authorized in 1869 for the North Fork from its mouth to Brashear's Salt Works, at the mouth of Leatherwood Creek, in Perry County. This work was done under commissioners who were directed to report to the Breathitt County Court. The slack water system undertaken by the Federal Government in 1880 was never extended 121 miles up the North Fork as recommended in various surveys. By the time dams and locks had been completed to Beattyville, the railroad had entered the North Fork Valley and had absorbed most of the traffic.

Push-boats, however, continued to ply the North Fork in its upper reaches after the railroad reached Jackson and until it was extended up the river to Hazard in 1913-14. During 1891-1914 Jackson rather than Beattyville was the distributing point of the upper Kentucky River Basin.

Going down the Kentucky on a boat or raft when the river permitted was also an accepted mode of passenger travel. During the early days it was the chief mode of travel into the Bluegrass and to the Ohio River towns. Even as late as the 1890's and 1900's every tide carried visitors out of the mountains. *The Jackson Hustler* of April 3, 1891, reported that four ladies en route from Whitesburg to Louisville were passengers on a boat going down the river picking up lumber. A week later the paper carried an item that several young men of the Jackson Academy "went down on rafts during the recent tide." A fascinating account of a trip from Jackson down the Kentucky River on a raft is included in John Fox, Jr.'s *Bluegrass and Rhododendron.*

Wilderness paths, some of them partly marked out by the Indian and the four-footed game of the forests, were used by the first settlers. They were narrow and could only be traveled on foot or on a horse. Where these paths were not clear or where they were not determined by a natural lay-out, trees and rocks were marked to note the route taken. This was done particularly at stream crossings, over divides, at turnings and retracings. Primitive wilderness paths sometimes developed from these marked routes. During the first period of settlement these paths were extended, more clearly marked, and partly improved by removing fallen tree trunks and large stones. This was the oxcart stage of roads. The first roads in this region were sponsored and under the management of the county court. Able-bodied men contributed so many days of road service each year to defray their taxes. This system, still in operation in some parts of the county, was a haphazard method of making and maintaining roads and was largely responsible for their poor condition.

In 1836 the State Legislature passed an act to establish a State road from the mouth of Troublesome Creek via Hazard to the Sounding (Pound) Gap of Cumberland Mountains. This road, it was stated, "would greatly promote the intercourse between the two states, and essentially conduce to the convenience and benefit of the population of the Country through which it would pass." An engineer was instructed by the act "to repair to that quarter, survey and locate an eligible route." At the time this act was passed Col. John Haddix was Perry County's representative in the State Legislature and it was through him that it was submitted and passed.

J. Green Trimble (*Recollections of Breathitt*) has given several interesting accounts of early roads:

> In the early part of the year 1837 my uncle, Solomon Cox, purchased a store in Mt. Sterling, embracing a variety of every department of merchandise, which was hauled in five wagons drawn by teams of from four to six horses to Hazel Green, thence down Holly creek to the Kentucky river at the mouth of War creek, which was then in Estill County. The State road from Mt. Sterling to Prestonsburg had been completed the previous year under an appropriation of $200,000 by the Kentucky Legislature, and the citizens living on the line between Hazel Green and the Kentucky river had finished a good wagon road the year before; and these were the first wagons that were ever seen on Holly creek. They were a great curiosity to many people who had never seen a wagon before, and it being Sunday many of the younger people followed the wagons several miles to the river.
>
> The goods were transferred from the wagons to push-boats and taken up the river to the mouth of Quicksand, which was then in Perry County . . . [p. 1] Thomas Sewell, being one of the leading merchants and one of the wealthiest men of the county, determined to have a good wagon road made into Jackson, so that he could receive good at all seasons of the year without having to rely upon the uncertain navigation of the river. So . . . principally at his own expense, and with a small appropriation from the county court, he made a good wagon road over the Pan Bowl mountain, striking the river at War Shoal, four miles below Jackson, then across the mountain to Frozen creek. The citizens living along the line on Frozen and Gilmore creeks completed the road to intersect with the State road two miles above Hazel Green. This road was used for the transportation of all freight taken to Breathitt County until the completion of the Lexington and Eastern railroad, about 20 years ago. [See pp. 18-19].

Mr. Trimble in his account (*Ibid.*, p. 18) of the funeral of Archibald Crawford, of Bear Creek, on the Middle Fork, during this period remarks that, "There were no buggies, as there were no buggy roads in the country at that time, and every one who attended either had to walk or go horseback . . ." He also remembered in his *Recollections* (p. 19) that Mr. A. T. (Dick) Wood, his next door neighbor in Mount Sterling for thirty-five years, drove the first six-horse team in Jackson in April, 1854. He continued to make this freight run until the outbreak of the War between the States.

Until more recent years roads in Breathitt County have been little more than bridle paths. Some of them even now would make difficult courses for the steeplechase. During a large part of the year they were impassable. The road up the Kentucky Valley was the last of the routes across the mountains to be improved by the State. Even after it became a "State road" it was little better than most county roads. Road materials and road "engineering" were inadequate.

Breathitt County today has only one macadamized road, State 15, which threads its way from Winchester, where it connects with US 60, through Jackson and Hazard to the Virginia line at Pound Gap. State 30, an improved highway, extends from Salyersville in adjoining Magoffin County through Jackson to Booneville, then through the southern end of Jackson County to East Bernstadt on US 25 in Laurel County. State 52, also an improved dirt road, extends from Jackson to Beattyville, Irvine, Richmond, and to the junction with US 62 at Boston in Nelson County. Busses now connect all these roads with larger cities, and trucking lines make regular runs through the county. County roads for the most part are still narrow and "seasonal." The road down the east side of the Middle Fork from its juncture with State 30 to Canoe is one of the better county roads.

The railroad more effectively penetrated the isolation of Breathitt County than all the roads and river improvements of the same period. The first line extended into the upper Kentucky Valley was the Kentucky Union, then familiarly known as the "K.U." Its first charter, granted in 1854, empowered the company to extend a line from Lexington to the Virginia border by way of the Kentucky River and Pound Gap. For thirty years the railroad remained on paper. In 1872 a new company under the same name was organized. Finally, between 1884 and 1886, Clay City, in the Red River Valley of Powell County, was connected by a short line with the Chesapeake & Ohio Railroad and thereby with Lexington. Between 1888 and 1890 the Kentucky Union was extended up the Red River Valley, crossed the North Fork at the mouth of Middle Fork, and then continued to Elkatawa, a few miles from Jackson in Breathitt County. On July 15, 1891, Jackson became the terminus of this road. The Lexington & Eastern Railroad Company was organized to succeed the Kentucky Union on October 13, 1891. In 1911 it was taken over by the Louisville & Nashville Railroad and the following year was extended up the North Fork to McRoberts in Letcher County. Since then it has been connected with lines leading through Pine Mountain by way of Pound Gap and the Breaks of the Big Sandy, and then to the eastern seaboard. As part of the L. & N. system the railroad through Breathitt County has connections with all the major railroad systems. The principal traffic over this line today is coal.

Another railroad line that played an important part in Breathitt's economic development during this boom period was the Ohio & Kentucky Railroad. It was started around 1899 at Jackson and by 1903 it had been extended from Jackson up Frozen Valley into Wolfe County. This line, known as the O. & K., passed through a region of profitable openings of cannel coal. It connected with the Lexington & Eastern at O. & K. Junction. In 1935 it was discontinued, and since then the tracks have been taken up and the beds have been converted into roads.

FIRST TRAVELERS

Long before the travels of Gist (see below) and the McAfee Company, hunters seeking pelts, adventurers exploring the land, and scouts seeking a way back into Virginia followed the two upper forks of the Kentucky River and thereby passed through the present territory of Breathitt County. Profits in the fur trade sent men into remote and dangerous parts of the western wilderness. Over half a century before the opening of Kentucky, articles suitable for trade with the Indians were transported across the mountains and floated down the Ohio to be exchanged for furs and skins. The Shawnee village of Eskippakithiki, mentioned by early Scottish traders as Little Pict Town, was located at Indian Old Fields, in what is now Clark County, from about 1718 to 1754. A trail used by French traders led from the Illinois River, crossed the Ohio near the mouth of the Kentucky, and passed by the site of Eskippakithiki. From there it continued on to Cumberland Gap and entered the country of the Cherokees in Carolina.

John Finley, on his trading voyage in the autumn of 1752, reached the Falls of the Ohio where frequent Indian encampments were held. On his return up the river he met at the mouth of Big Bone Lick a band of Shawnees who escorted him and helped transport his cargo of goods over an old trail up the Kentucky River to Eskippakithiki.

Hunters, traders, travelers, and early settlers alike tended to follow these old Indian paths as they had been largely determined by the best natural advantages of the country through which they passed. An ancient trace that branched off the Warriors' Path roughly followed the Kentucky River along its North Fork and passed through the area now embraced by Breathitt. It led on to "Sounding" (Pound) Gap which the Indians continued to visit as a hallowed hunting ground even after the coming of the

OXEN AND COAL SLED

first white settlers. Reminiscences of old-timers also suggest the possibility of other paths in Breathitt that were used by the Indians when they came into this area to hunt. One of these went up Frozen Creek and more than likely departed from the North Fork at the mouth of War Creek which it followed for a short distance. Another path led to Flint Mountain where, as the naming of the mountain would imply, the Indians obtained flint.

The route through Pound Gap, although of minor importance as an avenue of early immigration when compared with Cumberland Gap, opened into the important drainage basin of the Kentucky River, two miles from the headwaters of its longest and upper fork. It was one of the natural, if more difficult, arteries of travel. By following this North Fork of the Kentucky, and then the main river to its confluence with the Ohio at Carrollton, the traveler passed through 420 miles of varied country, ranging from the rugged Highlands of the Cumberland plateau to the rolling plains of the Bluegrass.

It is possible, although not too likely, that Dr. Walker, surveyor for the Loyal Land Company, touched points within the present territory of Breathitt County during his explorations in 1750. A careful study of his journal, together with an examination of the topography of the section, will show possibilities in several directions, including the South and Middle forks of the Kentucky River.

In the course followed in 1751 by the Ohio Land Company's scout, Christopher Gist, however, there is little if any doubt about his passage through Breathitt. Johnston, in his annotation of Gist's journal (*First Explorations of Kentucky*, p. 154) says: "Upon my theory that he passed ... from the waters of the Red River to those of the North Fork ... he would have encountered the country and laurel thickets described, and also coal in Wolfe and Breathitt counties then and afterward."

The two days, March 25 and 26, upon which Johnston makes this inference, Gist entered the following notation in his journal: "These two days we travelled thro Rocks and Mountains full of Laurel Thickets which we could hardly creep thro without cutting the way." (*Ibid.*, p. 154.) The following day, when Gist was more than likely still within the confines of Breathitt, he made this entry in his journal: "Our Horses and Selves were so tired we were obliged to stay this Day to rest, for We were unable to travel—On all Branches of the little Cuttaway River [North Fork] was Plenty of Coal some of which I brought into the Ohio Company." (*Ibid.*, p. 154) He continued along the North Fork and returned to Virginia by way of Pound Gap.

Daniel Boone wandered over and hunted in so much of Kentucky that legends of his sojourn in Breathitt County can be safely based on this fact alone. Until recent years there stood near the mouth of Frozen Creek a giant sycamore tree with a hollow trunk. The old people of this region claim that Daniel Boone and several other men who were with him stayed in this tree one night. According to this same story, they were nearly frozen to death and the next morning they decided to call the stream Frozen Creek. (The name "Frozen" according to another legend was given to the creek by some early settler or traveler who arrived in the region in the wintertime when the smooth-flowing water at its mouth was frozen).

The legend of Daniel Boone in Breathitt is partly supported by the naming of Boone's Fork of Frozen Creek, which is in the section where he is supposed to have hunted. Adams Birchfield, an early settler, told the story during his lifetime that when he first came into the county he found a hunter's camp on this branch of Frozen and on a near-by beech tree was carved the name of the great wilderness pathfinder, indicating that it was his camp. Daniel Boone or one of his companions also cut his name in the bark of another tree along the Thomas Strong Fork of Frozen Creek.

The McAfee brothers, who played a prominent part in the early settlement of the Bluegrass, came through the land of Breathitt on their way back to Virginia during the first part of August, 1773. Two of them, James and Robert, kept separate and sometimes contradictory journals of their trip up the Kentucky River and its North Fork. Although the entries in these journals are brief, they form the most complete of the early records of travel up this stream before the period of settlement in this area.

On August 6 this company, which also included another brother, George, a brother-in-law, James McCoun, Jr., and Samuel Adams, traveled twenty miles from a camping site on the North Fork, twelve miles above the mouth of the South Fork, and passed a "big creek" (Holly Creek) into the present territory of Breathitt. James wrote that there was "no good land still" and Robert commented on the "bad ground" which made travel difficult. At one point it was necessary for them to raft across the river. They camped that evening about six miles above the mouth of Frozen Creek. On the next day (August 7) they passed the mouth of Frozen Creek. James noted for the travel on this day that "Some good bottoms [were] seen—" and Robert wrote "'The River was something opener that we had good coming that day." The journey of this day brought them into the heart of present-day Breathitt. From a point of six miles above the mouth of Frozen Creek they followed the winding course of the river past the site upon which Jackson, Breathitt's county seat, was established sixty-seven years later. On the evening of the seventh they had reached the mouth of Quicksand, where they camped for the night.

On August 8 James remarked that "the hills were very high and full of greenbrier and some laurel," and Robert that "The river was very crooked so that we had to cross near 20 times and very often to our middle." The hills through here are so steep and so close to the river edge that it was often impossible for them to get a foothold, especially in the "bends." Neither of the McAfee brothers commented on Troublesome Creek, a large fork of the river which they passed on the morning of this day. They either had to ford Troublesome Creek or else pass its mouth on the western side of the North Fork. The difficulties of this day—the thick greenbrier and laurel bushes, and the repeated crossing and re-crossing of the river—probably obscured this event of the morning. Towards evening, when they had reached the present Breathitt-Perry line, James saw and brought down with his rifle a buck elk which supplied them with food the next four days. They camped on or near the spot of the killing and had a feast. On the ninth they entered the territory that is now embraced in Perry County.

After the McAfee brothers, hunters, alone or in groups, penetrated this same mountain wilderness, following the various forks of the Kentucky River and going up their tributaries in search of game. The first period of general settlement, beginning and ending with the Revolutionary War, brought around twelve thousand people into Kentucky. Many of these were great hunters who wandered over large sections of the State in search of fur-bearing game.

Aside from several possible settlements along Lost Fork and adjoining territory, in the 1780's, the next group of travelers or visitors of historical note in Breathitt were the patent surveyors. The James Reynolds patent or grant, issued in 1786, had been surveyed in 1784. The several patents held by James Ross and David Curry were surveyed in 1788. Other patents held in this region by Virginia veterans of the Revolution were surveyed around this time, although none of them, as far as is known, were taken up or in any way disposed of.

FIRST SETTLERS

In the process of frontier expansion the mountainous regions of western Virginia, Pennsylvania, and North Carolina were settled. Here the people developed a mountain culture based on log cabins, rifles, axes, hoes, stubborn independence, and a defense of the country from the Indians. On account of this background the mountainous section of eastern Kentucky was somewhat similar to the country which many if not most of the early settlers in the Kentucky Mountains had left. Furthermore, this region was not then considered as undesirable agriculturally as it later became in fact.

Settlement in the Cumberland Foothills

As settler after settler, alone or with his family and sometimes with friends, followed the traces along the meandering streams or took to the trails through narrow but fertile valleys, the foothills of the Cumberland Plateau began to assume more permanent aspects of human habitation. The well-to-do came on the small English stock horse then still common in the colonies. Most of the early settlers, especially men, walked while their horses and cattle were used as pack animals. When possible, the small children and then the women rode horseback. During the Revolutionary War hundreds of dwellers in the Allegheny valleys of the Old Dominion and North Carolina had packed up their most necessary belongings and traveled across the ridges. Here and there a thin, blue wisp of smoke rising above a small log cabin marked a lonely pioneer outpost in the wilderness. A plowed clearing, a hillside of peach seedlings or a row of bee-gums proclaimed the pioneer's new-found freedom. Now and then the forest echoed the hunter's rifleshot.

The Virginians and North Carolinians who took up

land claims along the Troublesome, the Quicksand, the Big Caney, and along the forks of the Kentucky River had undoubtedly been attracted by the rugged character of the land with its unexcelled virgin stands of timber, by the numerous streams, and the abundance of game, edible berries, and nuts. However, accidental reasons such as cold weather, exhaustion, the loss of one or more animals, and the presence of game for food, determined the settlement of land-seeking pioneers in the mountains. Otherwise, many of them would have gone on to the more desirable Bluegrass lands, already largely taken up and settled, or to more fertile tracts of western Kentucky.

As the difficulties of traveling were great, the first pioneers brought with them only the most essential objects. The pioneer was not complete without a weapon of some sort. In enumerating pioneer companies the chronicles often listed the number of guns as well as manpower, which was meaningless without a firearm to back it up. Bulky articles, even when they could have been "toted," made traveling slower and more difficult. For this reason they were left behind and either made or acquired after the homestead had been located.

The pioneer of necessity was somewhat of a craftsman. When he had picked out his piece of land, built or found a shelter, and planted his seed he then proceeded at his leisure to make the plain furniture of his home from the most elementary tools. He also shaped from native timber the wooden frame for the plow irons that he more than likely brought with him from the "old" settlement. Guns were brought for hunting and also for self-defense. The long-barreled flintlock and later the famed old Kentucky rifle were the most common. Occasionally a pioneer of more affluence also brought a fowling-piece. The bow and arrow, usually made from ash, hickory, cedar, and oak still survived from the Old World, but even at this time their use was largely confined to boys.

Seed with which to plant the first crop was as precious as gold to the prospective homesteader in the wilderness; and tools with which to till the soil and to build were as indispensable as a scalpel to a surgeon. The more fortunate had at least one pack horse and other stock, especially cattle. Dogs were often the pioneer's most serviceable companion. Hounds for hunting, for watchdogs, and as faithful animal companions were found in all well-equipped caravans.

In historical retrospect their efforts and deeds were adventurous, colorful, and sometimes dramatic, but to the men and women who participated in them they were often tedious and hazardous. Perhaps only the far-sighted and the imaginative sensed the historic importance of their generation. Visions of comfort and security, leavened by the spirit of freedom, gave the pioneers courage and hope. Their philosophy was a simple one; spun in home, arising from experience, and practical needs.

The Coming of the Nobles and Neaces

In the late summer or early fall of 1780, when the guns of the Revolution were still sounding along the seaboard and occasionally in the "backwoods," a group of young Virginians left one of the river valleys of the southwestern part of the Old Dominion. There was something of youthful romance and adventure in this party—all of them were under twenty years of age, and it is uncertain whether they had been married according to legal formalities. In those days, however, when frontier communities were far removed from the seats of law, plighted love was sufficient to tie the knot of wedlock.

For some time before their departure they had talked of moving west over the lofty cordons that marked the frontier outposts of that day. Earlier, in the autumn of 1779, they had evaded the marauding forces of the British troops then infesting the State by going farther to the west. They spent the spring and summer of the next year on the eastern slopes of the Appalachians.

In this pioneer band were the first settlers of Breathitt County: Nathan Noble and his wife, Virginia (Neace) Noble; William Noble and his wife; Enoch Noble, a brother of Nathan; Austin Neace and his wife, Malinda (Allen) Neace; and Henry Neace. All were bound together by ties of blood or marriage and all shared the same youthful expectations.

Although the narrative of their trek across the mountains varies in detail, and is based entirely on family tradition, it contains the intriguing elements, the romance and the lore of pioneering. According to one version the small colony of home-seeking Nobles and Neaces entered the State through Cumberland Gap in the wintertime. Here they were delayed two weeks by a big snowstorm.

According to another version of their journey into Kentucky, a version which is more detailed but no more probable, they left Virginia in late September and in early October had reached the upper waters of the Licking River. This route, across the mountains in a northwestern direction to the watershed of the Licking River and Quicksand Creek, was a more difficult and a much less traveled one than through Cumberland Gap. When they reached the mouth of Buckhorn and Troublesome (now in Perry County), a camp was established, and William Noble decided to make this the permanent home of his family. The entire party, with the exception of Nathan Noble and wife, Austin Neace and wife, and Enoch, Nathan's unmarried brother, decided to spend the winter with William Noble. Rock houses in the vicinity promised comfortable quarters, and there was plenty of game for food.

Nathan and his party took their leave of this camp early in November and journeyed down Troublesome to the mouth of Beaver Dam. Following the small stream to its head the party crossed over to Troublesome's Caney, and set up camp. Next morning the party turned up Caney to Cockrell's Fork of Lost Creek, another tributary of Troublesome. The journey then continued to a branch of Cockrell's Fork and down the fork to a point near its mouth where camp was set for the night.

It was already past the middle of November, 1780. Nathan's wife was soon to become a mother; and near by was found a rock house large enough to shelter the entire party. These were the urgent circumstances which determined the first settlement in Breathitt County—the hardships of winter, the approaching confinement of a young mother, and the availability of food and shelter. The colony prepared for the winter months. Nathan Noble, not being a hunter and not satisfied with the provisions of a cliff, set to work building a log hut for the winter large enough for the entire party. During the day he felled and prepared timber for the house. After his brother, Enoch, and Austin Neace returned from hunting, they helped to place the logs. Comfortable quarters were soon prepared.

FARM IN A HOLLOW

A large deer lick was discovered close by. When the weather permitted, ground was cleared and Austin started clearing and fencing land. He cleared a few acres and, by the first of June, they were planted in corn, beans, and in other garden seed which they had brought with them. This was undoubtedly the first garden grown in what is now Breathitt County. The other two men assisted in fencing the cleared ground, using rails split from easily cleaved timbers. It was planted surrounding the log cabin, where the hounds kept wild beasts from disturbing it. Here, late in the summer of 1782, Austin Neace's wife became a mother. Nathan Noble's wife had become a mother shortly after their settlement, but her child had died soon after birth.

After the first crop was planted, Nathan decided to make his permanent home about three miles below on Lost Creek, near its confluence with Leatherwood. At this point he had found the meadows broad and desirable. Nathan, assisted by the other men in the colony, erected his permanent log house here. Enoch, the hunter of this settlement, supplied the meat for his family and that of Nathan, who was the farmer and builder. Enoch spent his days roaming the forested hills, and returning with the choice game of the virgin land. At first he lived with his brother, but as their families increased and an additional room still left them crowded, Nathan built his brother a cabin about a half mile from his own. In the fall of 1782 these early Lost Creek settlers harvested enough corn, beans, pumpkins, and other vegetables to help carry them through the winter months and for planting in the following spring.

The small colony of Nobles and Neaces on Lost Creek and its tributary streams were an isolated community in an unmarked wilderness for over a decade. They fed on the plentiful game of the surrounding country and each year raised a vegetable garden and a crop of corn. It is probable during this time that one or more trips were made to the settlement at Clinch River or to one of the southwestern communities in Virginia. In the chronicle of the Nobles' settlement in the Kentucky Mountains there is mention of stone stew kettles used for making hominy; of the purchase of a salt kettle, an adz, and an outfit to make churns, water pails, barrels, and troughs, and a handmill for grinding corn. There is also mention of trips to Virginia with furs and ginseng, and of returning hunting parties. After the first settlement had been made, Jake Neace, a brother of Austin Neace and of Nathan's wife, and Samuel Allen, a brother of Malinda Allen Neace, Austin's wife, came into the county.

The Haddixes and Combses

After the entry of the Nobles and Neaces, the next settlement in the region that later became Breathitt County was made at the mouth of Troublesome Creek, in 1792. Samuel Haddix, the progenitor of all the Haddixes in the county, came from Clinch River, Virginia, during that year. His grandson, also named Samuel, in a letter to the *Jackson Hustler* in 1893 called this the "first settlement in Breathitt County," perhaps meaning the first settlement of the Haddixes. He wrote that there was not a foot of land cleared in the county at that time. The principal and most often the only food for a year was venison, since there was nothing of which to make bread nearer than Clinch River. In this party there was a trapper named Alex McQuinn, and a shoemaker by the name of Herman Hurst.

One of the oldest American families now residing in Breathitt was established in this section of the mountains by Harrison Combs, a descendant of one of the ten Combs brothers who came over from Scotland very early in Colonial history, most of them settling in Virginia. In 1795 Harrison Combs left Russell County, Virginia, with his ten-year-old son, Matthew. After "spying out" much of the land and hunting at the same time he finally settled in what was known as the "Big Bottom," about a half mile above the present site of Hazard. This was the first settlement along the North Fork of the Kentucky River in this section of Perry County.

Here Harrison Combs and his young son built a shanty to sleep in, cleared two acres of ground, and caught a young bear which they kept with them at their shanty. The young bear became Matthew's pet and stayed with them until it was large enough to eat. They had brought along with them corn and peach seeds, a rifle, and a supply of ammunition, an ax, a weeding hoe, an iron wedge, and a frow. As soon as they had planted some corn and had built their shanty, they returned to Virginia for the rest of the family. On the trip back they packed their household goods on two horses. The family walked and drove two cows.

The peach seed, planted in the "Big Bottom" around 1795, grew into such prolific fruit-bearing trees that their disposal became a problem. Harrison Combs, therefore, sent two of his sons, Matthew and Henry, to Washington County, Virginia, for a still. They hauled it to the foot of Black Mountain. There they took hickory withes and a sizable pole and carried it across the mountains to their home where it began a long and honorable career in the service of peach brandy. This still remained in the Combs family for many years.

Harrison Combs finally sold his homestead to his son, Matthew, and bought a farm on Troublesome Creek in the present territory of Breathitt County. The Troublesome Creek homestead was also sold to Matthew in 1828. Some time after Harrison Combs' first wife died, just about the time he sold out, he married a young woman and moved to the state of Indiana. He left behind him five boys: Matthew, Henry, Hugh, George, and Steve. The Troublesome Creek farm of Harrison Combs is still in the Combs family.

One of Matthew Combs' sons, Henry, figures prominently in the history of Breathitt County. His numerous children, some of whom gained a degree of prominence, and his many diversified activities make his name memorable. He became one of the most prosperous and farsighted farmers in this region, taking up a large section of virgin land on Troublesome Creek, comprising about 2,000 acres with about 25,000,000 feet of timber on it. He cleared much of this land and raised fine crops. By 1870 Henry Combs had planted on his farm 1,000 apple trees and ten acres of peaches, together with two acres of nursery stock for grafting purposes. He grew his cotton, ginned it, and the women on the place spun and wove it into clothing for the family. He made his own brick from clay on his farm, and he claimed to have made the first fireplace in this section of Breathitt County. He tanned leather and made shoes for all of his family, shaped on lasts made by himself. When any of his neighbors brought

46   *BREATHITT*

their own leather he made their shoes without charge, but usually they did some favor in return. Henry Combs had the reputation of making one shoe every night following his day's work on the farm. Henry Combs allso erected a schoolhouse on his place and hired a teacher. It was here that his children received their early education.

Later Settlers

During the last decade of the eighteenth and the first quarter of the nineteenth century, a group of several families whose surnames have the savor of old England in them, came from North Carolina to found new homes in the foothills of the Kentucky Mountains. Although it is possible that they came as early as 1790, only uncertain memories place the date of their entry into Kentucky this early. In this colony, which settled in the Middle Fork section, were the Spicers, Turners, Becknells, and Sebastians. With them or around the same time also came the Littles.

Many other settlers from North Carolina settled in the area now embraced by Breathitt County. James Johnson, who came with his two brothers, Israel and Frank, took up land on the Middle Fork at the mouth of Bollings Creek, while his brothers settled in Perry County. Another prominent family which settled along the Middle Fork and gave its name to a tributary creek was the Jetts. The progenitor of this family, Stephen Jett, came from Rappahannock River, near Richmond, Virginia. He first settled in what was then Fayette and later Bourbon County. Other families which settled along the Middle Fork included the Bryants, Terries, Crawfords, Aikmans, Amis', Evans', Arrowoods, Gabbards, Bakers, Bollings, Callahans, Heralds, and Griffiths.

William Hagins, descended from the North Irish Higgins', came from North Carolina and settled near the Spring Fork of Quicksand around 1840. Thomas, one of his five sons, built a two-story log house below the mouth of Spring Fork Creek, about fifteen miles southeast of Jackson. He held by proscription 3,000 acres of land from the head of Big Caney Creek to the mouth of Spring Fork, a distance of about nine miles. He was considered a man of wealth by the standards of that date, owning a number of slaves. Another son of William Hagins, Daniel, became prominent as sheriff of the county.

At a later date, Levi Hollan (Holland), who established another family which looms prominently in the affairs of Breathitt, came from North Carolina. The Cardwells of Breathitt trace their first settlement in the county to John Cardwell who immigrated from Knoxville, Tennessee, to the mouth of Panbowl Branch around 1830. His son, Thomas P., became active in Breathitt County politics, serving several terms in the State legislature (H.R., 1863-65, 1871-73, S.S., 1865-69).

Turners, Strongs, Combs', and Watts', in addition to the Nobles, Neaces, and Haddixes, settled along Lost Creek.

On Troublesome the Russells, Millers, Harveys, Allens, Campbells, Hayes', Richeys, Mulens', Hutsons, and Johnsons settled.

Along the North Fork there settled the Bohanons, Cardwells, Hargis', Sewells, Spencers, Souths, Hays', Spurlocks, Fraziers, Duffs, Hursts, Cockrells, Stidhams, Turners, Crawfords, Williams', Moores, Deatons, Aikmans', Amis', Whites, Shacklefords, Sheffields, and Chandlers.

Settlers on Quicksand included the Howards, Roberts', Millers, Pattons, Williams', McQuinns, Josephs, Manns, Bays, Patricks, Walkins', Keiths, Carpenters, and Crafts.

On Frozen Creek there settled families bearing the name of Cope, Day, Taulbee, Johnson, Pelfrey, Wilson, Bank, Flinchum, Shockey, and Hatton.

Outstanding among the families of German or Dutch origin who settled in Breathitt County are the Hursts, Kashes, Vancleves, and Bachs. Only the Bachs, who settled along Quicksand, and the Vancleves, who settled on Frozen Creek, have remained.

(Other early settlers and prominent families are mentioned elsewhere in this guidebook in connection with other stories.)

ESTABLISHMENT OF THE COUNTY AND ITS EARLY GOVERNMENT

The origin of Breathitt, like that of many if not most Kentucky counties, can be largely attributed to lack of roads and long distances counted by days from county seats. Confusion of land titles and the interminable land litigation of the State's early history constantly drew men to their county seats.

The only travel for many decades in large sections of the mountains was over narrow paths that of necessity crossed and recrossed streams and wended their ways over hills rugged with rocks, sometimes blocked by fallen trees and overgrown with the shoots of underbrush. Whenever settlers in distant parts of the county had business that called them to the county seat they had to plan on a trip, coming and going, from three to four days.

In the southern part of present-day Breathitt, forming part of Perry County's territory after 1820, it was necessary to travel as far as forty-five miles to Hazard for the recording of legal papers and to attend court sessions.

Simon Cockrell, Sr., one of the early settlers along the North Fork at its confluence with Boone's Fork, had to travel nearly fifty miles back and forth from Irvine, the seat of Estill County. This was a three-day trip over rugged country. As a large land and slave owner, which gave him the reputation of being the wealthiest man of his day in Estill and later Breathitt County, he often found it necessary to make this journey. Other settlers at even more distant points found the county seats remote, considered their interests neglected and, as was sometimes the case, their land rights outraged. It was out of such conditions that feeling arose for the formation of Breathitt County.

After some discussion among the most prominent

farmers of the Si Bend, Panbowl, and Quicksand sections, it was decided that the most forcible man among them was needed to carry through the proceedings necessary for the creation of a county. Jeremiah (Jerry) South, one of the early timbermen of the region, volunteered for this task. Jerry South, a native of Madison County, had taken up a tract of land in the fertile Panbowl section on the south side of the North Fork, two miles above Jackson. He married Millie Cockrell, daughter of John and niece of Simon Cockrell, Sr. From this it would appear that the Souths and Cockrells took a particularly active interest in the formation of Breathitt County.

Jeremiah South traveled over a large area in 1838 advertising and circulating the petitions for the formation of a new county to be called Breathitt. He then went to Frankfort where he approached the Kentucky Legislature. He performed all of these services without remuneration of any kind. Jeremiah South, for this initiative, has been deservedly named "The Father of Breathitt County."

The act establishing Breathitt County passed through the two houses of the legislature and was signed by Gov. James Clark on February 9, 1839. According to the provision of the act, however, Breathitt did not function as a separate unit of government until April 1, 1839. Its boundaries included portions which were later incorporated into four other counties. Owsley in 1843, Wolfe in 1860, Lee in 1870, and Knott in 1884 were given Breathitt territory. Perry, alone of the three counties from which Breathitt was formed, is still contiguous with its territory.

Its county seat, like that of practically all county seats, was centrally located so as to be equidistant to all parts of its jurisdiction. Three commissioners, John Speedsmith of Madison, Gabriel W. Price of Laurel, and Alexander Lackey of Floyd County were appointed by the Kentucky Legislature to locate a seat of government for the newly formed county of Breathitt. They first selected a beautiful and central location on the land of Nick Hays, opposite the mouth of Quicksand. A public square was marked off in an old peach orchard by driving down four stakes. Upon investigation, however, they found the title to this land defective. Rather than establish it through time-consuming litigation, they changed it to its present site, Jackson, which was then part of the farm of Simon Cockrell, Sr.

These commissioners were instructed by the act to make a report of their selection to the Breathitt County Court. Section 7 of the act erecting the county directed the justices to make provision for the purchase of a lot or lots suitable for the erection of a courthouse, jail, clerk's office, stray-pen, etc., and which they were to have erected as they thought necessary. Until these buildings were finished it was the duty of the county court, at the expense of the county, to procure a suitable house in which the sessions of the county and circuit courts could be held.

The act establishing Breathitt County provided for eleven justices of the peace who were to meet at the home of William Allen, at the mouth of Cane Creek, on the first Monday of April, 1839. In a letter to James M. Bullock, Secretary of State, dated February 22, 1839, Gov. James Clark nominated for his advice and consent as Justices of the Peace these eleven men: Stephen Jett, Hardin Combs, Alexander Herald, Jeremiah W. South, Thomas Higgins (Hagin), James P. Cope, Harman Hurst, Allen Moore, Simon Bohanon, Claiborn Crawford, and Andrew Pence. Richard South was nominated Sheriff and William Allen, Coroner of the newly-formed county of Breathitt. After taking their oaths of office and qualifying their sheriff, they were instructed to appoint a clerk. John S. Hargis was appointed first clerk of the Circuit Court and Simon Bohanon the first clerk of the County Court. Bohanon served only a short time. Upon his resignation John Hargis was appointed to fill the vacancy, and he held both offices for many years. Tax commissioners, appointed in 1839 by the Breathitt County Court, were governed by the laws then in force on the subject.

Six constables, to be appointed by the Justices of the Peace who constituted the county court, were instructed by the act to lay off the county into districts. Other constables were added and other constabulary districts were laid off in the next few years. One for the town of Breathitt (Jackson in 1845) was appointed in 1841, one for Holly, and one for Troublesome Creek, in 1846.

The Breathitt Circuit Court was first "holden" on the third Monday in April, July, and October as changed by

STIDHAM HOME, JACKSON

an enactment after the passage of the act creating the county which had previously set it on the third Monday in May, August, and November. Such matters as these were being continually changed by acts of the Kentucky General Assembly and by the State constitutions of 1850 and 1891. In his *Recollections* (p. 10), J. Green Trimble tells the story of the first circuit court held in the county:

> I attended the first term of the circuit court held in the county, which was held at the residence of Wm. Allen, on his farm at the mouth of Cane Creek, and with few exceptions, I attended every circuit court that was held in the county up to the beginning of the Civil War. Judge Joseph Eve was the presiding judge of the first court, and Silas Woodson represented the Commonwealth, and who at the request of the presiding judge, addressed the grand jury, giving the ablest instructions I ever heard delivered. Mr. Woodson afterwards emigrated to Missouri and located at St. Joseph, and was elected Governor of that State, one of the best that State ever had.

Among the early officials of the county, perhaps none were more influential and certainly none served longer than John Hargis. He was clerk of the county and circuit courts, representative of Breathitt and Morgan counties at the State's Third Constitutional Convention, and county school commissioner for a number of years, including the first years of the operation of public schools in Breathitt. Another official who served the county in these early years was Thomas Hagin (later spelling "Hagins") who was a trustee of Breathitt Town and sheriff of the county.

One of the most outlandish warrants issued during the early history of the State is the first one purportedly issued in Breathitt County. It is a priceless curiosity, even though it is of dubious origin and lacking in documentary background. It reads:

> I, Jackson Terry, Hi Official Magistrate, Squire and Justice of the Peace, do hereby issue the following rit against Henderson Harris, charging him assault and battery and the breach of the peace on his bruthern law, Tom Fox by name: This warrant cuses him of kickin, bitin and scratchin and thron rocks and doin everything that was mean and contrary to the Law in the state of Jetts Creek and aforesed.
> This warnt otherwise the Hi Constable, Miles Terry, by name to go forthwith and forthcomin and rest the said Henderson Harris and bring him to be with accordin to the law of Jetts Creek and

aforesed. This warnt otherwise the Hi Constable to take him where he finds him on the hillside as well as in the level, to take him where he aint as well as where he is and bring him to be delt with accordin to the laws of Jetts Creek and aforesed.

[Signed] JACKSON TERRY

Hig Constable, Magistrit and Squire and Justis of the Peace of the State of Jetts Creek aforesed

John Breathitt (1786-1834), the county's namesake, was a school teacher, surveyor, lawyer, state legislator, and Governor. By his thrift and industry he acquired considerable property consisting mostly of lands. He was twice married and had three children. When he died on February 21, 1834, after serving as Governor of Kentucky from 1832, he was well on his way to a career of greater public honor. In 1800 his father, William Breathitt, removed from Virginia where John, the eldest of his five sons and four daughters, was born. Although he took up several small tracts of land in Logan County, Kentucky, and owned a few slaves, he did not have sufficient wealth to send his children away to school. John made the most of his scant opportunities for schooling, and by diligent study of the books within his grasp made himself a good surveyor. He was appointed a deputy surveyor of public lands before he became of age. He read law under Judge Caleb Wallace, of Woodford County, and was admitted to the bar in 1810. In a short time he had built up a lucrative law practice. He was known for his courtesy to all and was popular in political and law circles. In 1811 he was elected Logan County's representative to the State Legislature and in this capacity served until 1815. In 1828 he was elected Lieutenant Governor of Kentucky. Politically, he was an ardent supporter and a great favorite of the Democratic party. He warmly espoused the election of General Jackson to the Presidency in 1828 and again in 1832. His success in accumulating wealth enabled him to help his father in liberally educating his brothers and sisters.

THE EARLY FEUDS OF "BLOODY BREATHITT"

The reader who dips into the tales of the clan and border wars of Scotland is apt to find particularly appealing certain qualities of romance and adventure. Prosper Merimee's *Colomba,* a vehicle for teaching college French, has revealed to innumerable American students something of the strange code and blood-tingling danger of a Corsican vendetta. Yet the numerous feuds that have taken place on the Appalachian fringes, akin in many respects to the Scotch border wars and the Corsican vendettas, have never been looked upon or treated as romances or adventures. Distance has not lent them that enchantment.

Nevertheless, many of the mountain feuds have the copious detail and the moral shadings that make a comprehensive account the only balanced one. When taken seriously, they have too often been approached from a sociological rather than a historical point of view and, when treated lightly, they have been tritely satirized or put into such ballads as "Tin-Pan Alley's" delightful fiction of the "feudin' of the Martins and Coys." John Fox, Jr., is the only well-known author who has presented the feuds in a truthful yet imaginative manner, but his wooden style and his limited plots have ruled out the myriad nuances that give color and deepen the interest of every major feud.

Sensationalism, moral indignation, and discreet silence have each veiled one large aspect of the feuds. In reality they are complex and difficult for the outsider to understand. Perhaps no other phase of American civilization can give us events and characters which, with their Anglo-Saxon variations, suggest the events and characters found in certain Russian novels, particularly those of Dostoevski. They can be properly understood only in terms of the psychology of men in an environment highly conducive to family dislikes, overheated political contentions, the swilling of considerable quantities of liquor, free gunplay, and the brooding desire for revenge.

It was inevitable in a particularly hilly country where ridges and creeks tended to mark off one clan and its supporting faction from another, and where Mother Nature was hostile and niggardly that blood ties would be particularly strong and that feudal ties between men should develop. For this reason, what was equivalent to a tribal spirit sometimes arose in these sharply defined communities. Those forms of social organization, that in a more populous and more developed society break up what we may term the clan, did not exist in most of the mountain sections of Kentucky. The blood ties and the clan or factional interests were real; they were present in day-to-day living, represented the individual's well-being, and offered him the little that could be expected of life in the region. Outside the clan and faction the individual stood alone.

The feuds of Breathitt originated in the depredations that occurred during and for a short time after the War between the States. It is important to remember in this connection that Breathitt is a "border" mountain county where there was a sharp division in sentiment between the North and South. The antagonisms that sprang up then lived on long after their first causes had been forgotten.

Often the particular incident that has caused a long smoldering feud to flare up has been of a simple and trifling nature—a quarrel over politics, some business or personal matter, or sudden, revenge-seeking anger during a game of cards. One of the feuds of Breathitt, involving the death of many men and years of malice, is even said to have started over a stolen watermelon. Although an apocryphal story, it is an incident no more trivial than others more authentic. Then, in a region where the local law enforcing agencies have been weak and oftentimes controlled by a hostile faction, where the county is large and the people scattered, where the central authority is not always immediately available and, perhaps, like the district justice of the peace, reluctant to act in a decisive manner or indifferent to the formal aspects of justice, the mountaineer readily resorts to the private avenging of wrongs. It has been his grudging surrender of avenging wrongs to the law and the widely current disbelief in its impartiality among all mountaineers that has kept the feud spirit alive. This, more than any other single cause, explains the frequent use of the ambush in the mountain feuds.

The mountaineer does not always seek justice immediately, but will wait for years for the opportune moment. He follows the old Hebrew dictate, "An eye for an eye and a tooth for a tooth." Just as he is "a good lover, a character who never forgets his benefactor," as W. R. Thomas has called him in *Life Among the Hills and Mountains of Kentucky* (pp. 88-89), so he is also a fierce hater. "He never forgets an injury or injustice perpetrated against him, and it rankles in his breast as long as his heart beats. Consequently, revenge is the sweetest morsel he can roll under his tongue. He must have this revenge ..."

When a feud, recognized as such, has entered a particularly active stage, both factions realize that they must win, give up, if possible, or be wiped out. Neither side, therefore, considers the ambush and other stealthy methods of wiping out their enemy as cowardly. In this sense old frontier values lingered on in the Southern Appalachians after they had become outmoded throughout most of the country. Men of a feuding faction went armed, often accompanied by other armed men, and they kept to friendly paths. If the other side did ambush one of their men in this manner, they did not depend on the law for revenge, and usually they did not cry out, "dirty, cowardly work"—they simply set out to do likewise. Half-beaten enemies are likely to seek terrible and treacherous revenge.

In the estimates of different men who have figured in the feuds, it becomes strikingly evident that many of them were caught by circumstances and were unequal to the task of opposing a rigid, almost sacred code. One is apt to remark of a prominent man who had seemed to be a good citizen, a kindly individual, a hard worker, and a family man, "Do you mean that he was mixed up with the feud?" The answer will usually be something like this: "Yes, he couldn't help it. After all, he's human and what else could he have done?" Some of the men who were involved, or on the brink of being involved in a feud, left the county. Sometimes the estimates of some particular figure, such as Captain Strong, are so contradictory that it becomes evident that each of them has an element of truth. Even the colors of a feud are not all black and white. However, many of the men who took an active part in the feuds were bad characters with few redeeming qualities. The feud gunmen took lives with the same ease that they ate their grits, pork, and corn pone. The leaders with an equal ease have entered into conspiracies, marked men for assassination, and bought or intimidated juries.

The hills of "Bloody Breathitt," as other impoverished rural communities, whether in the mountains or not, are peopled in the main with simple, right-living folk. Contrary to any implications otherwise, they are not insensible to moral values. It is true that some of the people in Breathitt, after a shooting, might ask "How big a hole did it make?" — as one newspaper correspondent reported — but that morbid remark is not their primary interest. It is one of the remarks of curiosity that might be shown by anyone—anywhere. In Breathitt it is also true, as Horace Kephart in *Our Southern Highlanders* reported a mountain judge as saying, many years ago, that "Hit used to be that when a man killed another, all his friends rushed in an went on his bail. But now the sympathy's all with the corpse." If a few have not regarded the taking of another's life as heinous a crime as others who are favored with a greater degree of moral consciousness, then it can be said, not in justification but in extenuation, that they have progressed no further in a society of "rugged individualists" than nations have in the world order. The overwhelming majority of the people of "Bloody Breathitt" are as unsensational as some few of its feud leaders and feud killers have been found sensational.

The Bushwhacking Origin of Breathitt's Feuds

One morning during the War between the States, according to fireside feud-lore, a group of armed men were driving a small herd of cattle, a drove of hogs, and a few sheep down a creek bed in Owsley, a county bordering Breathitt. At their head was old Dan Aikman calling out to the stock in a shrill voice that echoed through the pinched valley and resounded from the craggy summits of the enclosing hills. Suddenly the bleating, grunting and mooing of the drove was stilled with the whine of a bullet from an overlooking ridge. Then a shower of lead sent the men scurrying to shelter. Only old **Dan Aikman**, hard of hearing and unmindful of the danger, continued on his way calling out to the cattle, hogs, and sheep behind him. The other men returned gunfire from the comparative safety of tree trunks and the thick foliage of underbrush. Tradition does not relate whether any of these armed drovers were wounded or killed—merely that two of them who figure in the feud annals of Breathitt were unharmed. Soon they passed out of the firing range of the "hog" rifles of the embattled hill farmers and continued downstream. Old Dan was still blissfully and heedlessly calling out to the stock, and his partners resumed their work of scouring the territory for cattle, hogs, sheep, and work animals.

These men, led by Dan Aikman and Jerry Callahan, were Union bushwhackers collaborating in pillage with Breathitt's earliest feud chieftain, Bill Strong, captain of Company K of the "Greasy" Fourteenth, a Union regiment of volunteer Kentucky cavalry commanded by Col. H. C. Lilly. Shortly after this incident Aikman, Callahan, and their men crossed into Breathitt County, the base of their so-called "home guard" activities. Here they soon stumbled across some disconcerting news and they quickly headed back into Owsley County, holding on to their newly acquired wealth and keeping safely out of Strong's reach.

Two of Captain Strong's henchmen, as they were informed, had made the mistake of quarreling with him over the division of the plunder. One of these was Wiley Amis, a second lieutenant in Company I, captained by Thomas Amis, and the other was Wilson Callahan, the father of Jerry Callahan, who is not recorded as belonging to any military organization. Wiley Amis, with his party of men, had been "covering" the northern half of the county, including the county seat, while Captain Strong, together with Wilson Callahan, several of the Amises, and their followers were skimming the cream off the Lost Creek section. The pillaging expeditions that took place at this time have since been known as "the cattle war," since the principal booty was cattle.

Before setting out they had agreed to bring their loot to a certain point where another member of the Amis clan was keeping guard. Therefore, when the detachments under Amis and Strong had completed the pillage in their respective sections, they returned and proceeded to divide the spoils of profitable patriotism. Captain Strong, it is said, demanded and took the lion's share. This angered the Amises and Wilson Callahan, and they shortly afterwards became undying foes of Strong and his men.

This incident began the Strong-Amis feud which wracked Breathitt County for almost a decade. The Amises, who settled on Long's Creek in Breathitt County during the late 1830's, came from near-by Clay County. They were well, probably all too well, represented in the Fourteenth Cavalry for Captain Strong's schemes. The feud between this clan and their supporters and Captain Strong and his band finally "burned itself out" when John Amis, the leader of his faction, was killed in 1873, and the other Amises, not yet dead, left for Missouri.

During the dark days following the war—days when there was often no county coroner—days partly obliterated in the stealth of a night around 1873 when the county's official records went up in flame—the memories of living men and the stories handed down in some of Breathitt's old families relate a cruel, insidious war of half-concealed hate and revenge. Captain Strong, due to his military prerogatives in the war and his feudal presumptions afterwards, was one of the strongest and most influential men in Breathitt. He attempted to wield great and often merciless authority for many years, though not always successful. It is said that he conducted court-martials and condemned to death those who displeased him or challenged his right to hold the scepter of lordly sway over the realm of Breathitt. Such a court-martial, it is said, condemned Wilson Callahan, John Amis, and perhaps other members of the clan. But execution did not take place for a long time and then it was not before a firing-squad; nor was any evidence submitted or a plea for life entertained. Assassins were chosen and, at some

SHEEP IDYLL

favorable opportunity, the men that Strong had marked years before were ambushed.

Strong's Coup d'Etat and Breathitt's First Military Occupation

In the middle seventies a series of events forming a more definite picture in Breathitt's feud history led to the dispatch of State militiamen to Jackson for the first time in the history of the county. The troubles involved not only the Littles and Jetts, whose names the opening chapter of this feud now bears, but also the Cockrells and, as always, Capt. Bill Strong.

Some time around 1874 the afterwards notorious Jerry Little spread an unsavory and perhaps unfounded rumor about one of the daughters of James Cockrell. This young lady's brothers naturally proceeded to avenge her honor. An even more serious incident occurred around the same time when Jerry Little shot and killed Curtis Jett, Jr., in some quick-trigger action near the courthouse in Jackson. In return, Jerry Little received a load of buckshot from Curtis Jett's brother, Hiram. These two brothers were sons of Curtis Jett, Sr., who at that time was probably Breathitt's most prominent merchant-farmer. This fray with Jerry Little caused the Jetts to ally themselves with the Cockrells against the Littles. In the meantime, David Flinchum had killed a Negro, and Bill Strong, the special protector of the colored race in Breathitt, went on the warpath and took service in the Little army. The Flinchums joined the Cockrells for protection. By the time all these incidents had occurred, the outlines of the war had been clearly defined, and hostilities opened in earnest with casualties on each side. Then, one day Captain Bill, probably smarting under political reverses in election campaigns after the war, and no doubt hungering for some of his old power, performed a coup d'etat. He took over the courthouse in Jackson.

The county officials thereupon appealed to the Governor for reinstatement and protection. Sixty State Guards left Louisville for the seat of the war on the sixteenth of September, 1874. When the insurrectionists heard, a little more than an hour before their arrival, that troops were bearing down upon them, they scurried to their mountain homes. The number of guards was later increased until five companies of militia were gathered at Jackson, where they remained until and through part of December, protecting the court in the discharge of its duty. The casualties of military occupation at this time consisted of one soldier killed and one wounded by the accidental discharge of a comrade's gun.

The settlement of the particular enmity between the Littles and Jetts somewhat lightens the feud history of Breathitt. Two years or so after the gunplay between these two clans, High Sheriff John Linville Hagins, a young man of twenty-six or thereabouts, was instructed by County Judge James Back to arrest those involved in the shooting and bring them to court. The high sheriff, knowing as friends many of the men engaged on each side, attempted to bring the feud between the Jetts and Littles to an end without any more bloodshed or stirring up any more hatred. He went to Hiram Jett and said, "I have come to arrest you, Hiram, and would like for you to come peaceably." Jett replied, "I'll go if Little will." Sheriff Hagins then went to see Jerry Little, whom Jett had shot but not killed, and said, "I've come alone to arrest you. Will you come peaceably?" Little agreed to arrest provided the Jetts would also submit. The following day Sheriff Hagins went after the Littles and his deputy went after the Jetts. Deputy Sheriff Back was with the Jett faction in the courtroom when Hagins reached there with the Little faction, and both were brought in without a gun. The court then took bond for their appearance at the next term of circuit court.

Hiram Jett, like so many men who have been involved in feuds by family ties and seemingly unavoidable incidents, was an upstanding gentleman. He had the good sense to be persuaded to move to Madison County, where he lived until his death and where he and his wife reared their family. A romantic sequel to the Little-Jett feud was the marriage in 1899 of ex-Sheriff John Linville Hagins to the widow of Hiram Jett.

One of the incidents in the strife between the Cockrells and Littles at this time gives an idea of the relentless nature of feudal hatreds. Logan Cockrell was killed in gunplay between the factions one day. Jerry Little was badly wounded and, seeing that he was in a critical situation, he fled to the river a short distance away. There was a heavy drift near by and he sought safety here. His pursuers trailed him by the blood from his wounds. When they had reached the river where he had waded in, Jerry had placed his head between the logs above the water and had made a cover of drift branches to hide himself His pursuers searched up and down the river for a mile on both sides looking for the place where he might have come out. Finally, they concluded he had drowned and they gave up the search. Little stayed in the river until dark and then quietly swam across and stole his way home.

Little-Burnett Feud: Elections of 1878

The Little-Burnett feud, the first to receive Nation-wide publicity, was named for the principal characters in the incident which brought it to a dramatic pitch. It was hailed as "Another War in Breathitt" by the press of the country, which was following the lead of Kentucky papers already acquainted with the war-engendered lawlessness in the county. Captain Strong was castigated in a one-column subhead of the Louisville *Courier-Journal* as "A Loyal Whangdoodle," and he was cited with no mincing of words as the "Wonderful Effect of the Firing on Fort Sumter . . . ."

Eighteen hundred and seventy-eight was that ominous anno Domini—an election year. Among the aspirants for the important office of county judge · were former Judge E. C. Strong, who was a cousin of Capt. Bill Strong, former Judge D. K. Butler, and John Wesley Burnett, a member of the county bar. All were candidates for the Democratic nomination, and they actively canvassed the county until the opening of the June county court, when a one-day party convention was to be held in Jackson. Much bitterness had already been stirred up when the "unterrified" assembled to select their party nominees. The devil himself was loosed in no time at all. Large quantities of applejack had been sent gurgling down many throats. Pistols were fired into the air with the staccato of a western movie. It was not the "wild and woolly West," though, but only the otherwise quiet hamlet of Jackson on convention day. The Democratic gathering broke up in a general row without accomplishing anything except an increase in the warlike feeling already existing. The campaign had been warm before, and now it became "hotter'n hell." Butler withdrew, leaving the field to Burnett and "Red Ned," as E. C. Strong was known. The Republicans did not put up a candidate, but simply picked out the side that suited their individual preferences or their health.

Young Burnett was engaged to Evaline Cockrell and he was a frequent visitor at the Cockrell home. Since there was enmity between the Cockrells and Littles, Burnett was considered a Cockrell partisan. The Littles, a large and prominent family but often politically divided, supported ex-Judge Strong. Capt. Bill Strong went against his old enemies, the Littles, thereby deserting his cousin Ed who, for all his shrewdness, the captain considered too soft for the warlike business of politics and feud government. Big John Aikman, Bill Strong's bitterest enemy, allied himself with the Littles and supported "Red Ned." J. C. B. (Whick) Allen, a justice of the peace who later played a prominent part in the battles that followed, was also a follower of "Red Ned" and a supporter of the Little faction.

As the day of election drew near in August, there was a feeling that something would happen. Burnett, drawing his support from the more law-abiding element, was advised by some of his friends to withdraw, as Judge Butler had done, and let "Red Ned" have the election by default. This he refused to do, insisting that he must discharge his duty. The election, however, was held without violence.

After the board of canvassers had counted the vote, Burnett was declared victor by the narrow margin of eight votes. His opposition openly swore that he should never assume the duties of office to which he had been elected. Judge Burnett took his certificate and, with three friends, rode day and night until he reached the Governor's Mansion in Frankfort, where he applied for his commission. The Governor became suspicious of such an extraordinary procedure and decided it would be wiser to withhold the commission until he heard from the clerk and sheriff of Breathitt County and promised Burnett to forward his commission within two weeks if everything proved to be in order. Judge Burnett was satisfied with the Governor's course and he admitted his action was not according to custom, but explained that he had risked his life in the election and did not want to run any risks of having his victory stolen by some trick. He received the commission within the time specified and was installed in office without mishap.

The narrowness of Burnett's election and his trip to Frankfort further inflamed the feelings of Judge Strong's supporters, although Strong himself accepted the situation and retired to his home on Lost Creek. It is related that at a Baptist association in the county, after the August elections, ten or twelve of "Red Ned's" followers, headed by Big John Aikman, were moving toward an attempt on Judge Burnett's life, but his friends rallied to his support and the party withdrew without any bloodshed. On two other occasions Ned Marcum's house in Jackson, where Burnett boarded, was attacked with gunfire.

Disinterment of Jason Little's Wife

In the meantime, other events equally foreboding were weaving themselves into this pattern. A sordid murder, the prominence and aggressiveness of the suspect's people, and the open defiance of constituted authority played a more direct part in the Little-Burnett feud than the election. After he had been installed in the office, Burnett was informed that the wife of Jason Little, an uncle of the already mentioned Jerry Little, had died and had been buried beneath her husband's house under strange circumstances. Judge Burnett thereupon ordered the body disinterred and Isaac Terry to act as county coroner and determine with the aid of a jury the cause of the woman's death. The coroner and his jurors, together with a number of guards, cautiously entered his premises. They raised her body and discovered gunshot wounds stuffed with beeswax. The inquest also revealed that the murdered woman was soon to become a mother. Sheriff Hagins arrested Jason Little and a charge of murder was placed against him. The court then ordered him to be secretly taken to the Fayette County Jail in Lexington, for the jail in Jackson was not safe enough to protect him against those who would mob him or against his relatives and friends who would release him.

Some time before the Breathitt Circuit Court convened, on November 25, 1878, Deputy Sheriff Charles Jefferson Little, a blood-kinsman of the man indicted for murder, went before Circuit Judge Randall, then presiding at Hazard in adjoining Perry County, and procured an order directing the return of the prisoner from Lexington before the convening of court in Jackson. This was a step seemingly meant to provide an escape for the prisoner. The deputy sheriff quickly gathered a body of his friends to help him execute the order. They mounted swift steeds and galloped to the head of the Coal Road in Montgomery County, the nearest railroad point. High Sheriff Hagins, who lived on Quicksand, was immediately informed of what was happening. He summoned a posse and headed in hot haste to the railroad. The deputy and his group were still there awaiting the train, and when it came both parties boarded it. In Lexington each group, after reaching the jailer's home, demanded the prisoner, but the jailer delivered him to the high sheriff. Each party returned on the same train to the head of the Coal Road, again mounted their horses, and headed towards Jackson. Since the deputy sheriff and his men were unhampered with a prisoner, they made better time and rode day and night, reaching town a day or so before the high sheriff with his posse and prisoner. Sheriff Hagins and his men took a more devious route for fear of ambush or an open attempt to take their prisoner.

Jackson Puts on Its War Paint

While Hagins and his men were cautiously making their way through rock-bestrewn passes, and fording streams swirling with ice cold water, Jackson was putting on its war paint. In anticipation either of the court session and its accompanying festivities or of an approaching conflict, the Littles, who lived near Jackson, brought in a barrel of apple brandy Sunday night, November 24. Early Monday morning, Bill Strong and his band arrived and stacked their larger arms in a vacant log building about a hundred yards from the courthouse, and then sauntered out upon the street wearing only their sidearms. In Strong's band of desperadoes were "Nigger Dick" Strong, former slave of Strong's father, the two quadroons, William and Daniel Freeman, Hen Kilburn, Steve McIntosh and seven or eight others. On the opposing side were the Littles, Allens, Gambles and the star gunman of the faction, Big John Aikman. Circuit Judge William Randall opened court that morning, delivered his charge to the grand jury, and then adjourned court until after dinner.

Before the court reassembled, Big John Aikman, with a band of about a dozen well-armed men, dashed into town. Captain Strong and his men were standing on the street in front of Breeding's store. Horses were hitched, and for a moment there was a strained silence. Then one of the Freeman Negroes is said to have stepped up to Big John Aikman and asked him, somewhat impudently, what he wanted. Aikman, in his weirdly humorous manner, smiled, drew out his .32 and answered in a stream of profanity that he would "take a dead nigger." This set off a brief but general exchange of fire between the two bands. Only William and Daniel Freeman fell at this time. Daniel was shot in the back and the lead went through his right side.

Strong's band withdrew to the log cabin where they had stacked their guns. Aikman and Justice of the Peace Allen reportedly stood their ground for awhile, peppering the fugitives with shot, and then they retired to the courthouse where they established their headquarters. From the courthouse and the log-cabin barricades an ineffectual but fairly regular fire was kept up until nightfall. Daniel Freeman, who was left lying in the street for nearly two hours, slowly dying, was removed and taken to the Haddixes, near the mouth of Troublesome Creek, seven miles from Jackson, where he died. William, who recovered, was able to ride home.

When hostilities broke out between the Aikman and Strong parties, the streets of the town were deserted. Men, women, and children fled to the safety of their homes, and many of the out-of-towners sought safety in stores or near-by barns. Under cover of darkness, they crept out of their places of refuge and hastened out of the town and to their homes. That night Aikman withdrew from the courthouse to Alfred Little's house, down by the river, while Strong still held his fort and awaited developments. Upon the arrival of Deputy Sheriff C. J. Little's posse, without his kinsman-prisoner, Jason Little, the little town again became tense with dire expectation. There was a rumor that plans had been made to rescue the prisoner, another that a mob desiring to wreak vengeance on the heartless wife-murderer had laid an ambush and were going to force the high sheriff to turn the prisoner over to them. These rumors and the fact that there was a large number of the prisoner's relatives among Aikman's "storm troopers" put the town on edge.

Jason Little Is Returned to Jackson

High Sheriff Hagins and his posse of ten men were expected on Tuesday morning. Judge Randall ordered Deputy Sheriff James Back to get together a posse of fifteen men and reinforce the sheriff. Judge Burnett, among the first to offer their services, took over the leadership of the posse. A particular friend of Burnett's tried to prevent him from going by reminding him that he was a marked man, but the judge insisted on going and said that, since he expected to be killed anyway, he would like to fall as an officer should—in the discharge of his duty. The two posses met at Twin Creek, about five miles from town. When they approached Jackson, near the ferry, they were signaled to ride further down the river in order to avoid trouble.

Aikman, seeing the turn that affairs were taking, declined to participate in the attempted rescue expected by all. He thereupon saddled his horse and headed home. A short distance from town, he hailed the deputy's posse and said, "Look out, or you will catch hell when you go back to town, for they are going to take the prisoner from you."

After Aikman's desertion, "Squire" Allen took over the command of the Little army which had been reinforced by other friends until it numbered around fifty men. It was a dangerous and irresponsible corps crazed with drink and excitement. The barrel of applejack brought in by the Littles had been going down steadily.

The sheriff and his mounted posse, now numbering about twenty-seven well-armed men, slowly made their way into town in the middle of the afternoon on Tuesday, November 26. Jason Little was taken to the little weather-

BOY WITH A BULL-TONGUE PLOW

boarded log jail, and the guard returned to the street where they began to disperse, thinking the danger was over at this particular time.

Assassination of Judge Burnett and Tom Little

As Judge Burnett was walking from the jail toward his boarding-house, two members of the Little faction, a Campbell and a Little, unexpectedly started berating him and threatening to take his life. Confusion followed. It is related that insulting, challenging, threatening remarks were shouted back and forth. Judge Burnett, however, did not tarry but kept walking, Sheriff Hagins by his side. Then, it seems, a volley was poured out in the direction of the dispersing guard who, taken by surprise, sought the nearest shelter. Someone shouted to Judge Burnett: "Watch out!" The young judge turned around and a shot, said to have been fired by Alfred Gamble, came from behind a little soda fountain (*sic*) where the Hargis Bank Building now stands, and lodged in Burnett's chest. Sheriff Hagins, it is reported, also turned around in time to see Alfred Little, a nephew of Jason Little, standing beside Gamble with his gun pointed at him (Hagins) ready to fire. When he pulled the trigger, however, it snapped and, in failing to fire, Hagins' life was saved. Judge Burnett ran fifteen or twenty steps up the street, faltered, and then fell in front of the George W. Sewell home. He was picked up and carried into the house where he died fifteen minutes later.

While the picket firing was going on, the band under "Squire" Allen rushed the jail and started battering the doors with axes. Tom Little, of Campton in adjoining Wolfe County, a brother of Jerry Little and a cousin of the prisoner, came up and entreated them to give up their jail-breaking, but in the midst of his plea he was suddenly shot.

"Mob Law" Rules Over Jackson

The fall of Mr. Tom Little greatly shocked everyone, so much so that the attempt to rescue Jason Little was immediately abandoned. The three parties withdrew to their separate barricades, Strong to his fort, Allen to the courthouse, and the sheriff and guard to the hotel facing the jail. Night soon put an end to the battle. The Allen party, under the cover of darkness, deserted the courthouse, finished off the applejack, and left town early Wednesday morning. The sheriff and posse thereupon took possession of the courthouse and thereby commanded the door of the jail, while Captain Strong and his men marched off to their homes up the North Fork.

Conditions in Jackson were reported to have been frightful after the shooting of Judge Burnett and Tom Little. The town was literally at the mercy of a mob, with the law at bay in a small wooden hotel and later in the courthouse. Reputable people left the town as soon as they could safely get out. Capt. R. S. Cheves, editor of the *Mt. Sterling Democrat,* wrote on November 27 that men were "drunk and wild with frenzy, armed to the teeth, with pistols, and guns," and that they were "walking the streets yelling at the top of their voices, proclaiming who they intend to kill." To make the break-down of law and order even more complete, Judge Randall suddenly disappeared on Wednesday morning before seven o'clock without leaving any orders or instructions.

If conditions were as chaotic as described by Captain Cheves, they quieted down in the following days. When the Governor's messenger, Lieutenant Thompson of the State Guard, visited Jackson on December 7, he reported "everything quiet . . . no war or rumors of war," and that the people were proceeding with their business. "The excitement was nothing like so great as reported, and did not extend to the people generally."

Troops and Trials Bring Peace to Breathitt

Governor McCreary was inclined to minimize the seriousness of the situation as reported in the newspapers. He learned afterwards in correspondence with Randall that if a special term of court were to be held in Jackson the judge would preside only with the protection of State troops. Therefore, in the middle of December, 1878, for the second time within half a decade, troops were ordered to Breathitt County. Up until December 23, 1878, the time previously announced by Randall for the convening of a special court, his whereabouts were generally unknown. Even Sheriff Hagins was uninformed, and shortly before the opening of the trials he sent out a messenger to locate him.

Many of those who participated in the crimes committed during the grave disorders were arrested, and about twenty of those indicted were taken to Louisville and confined in the Jefferson County Jail. They were brought back to Jackson the following summer by a military escort that remained on duty three weeks until the completion of their trials. Jason Little was tried for the murder of his wife during this court and found guilty. The intervention of friends succeeded in getting a sentence of life instead of death. He was sent to the penitentiary in Frankfort, and after serving some years was pardoned. The troops sent to Jackson in December remained on duty until the middle of February, 1878.

Some of the men involved in the November riots fled to remote, almost inaccessible hiding places. A few later gave themselves up to the civil authorities of the county when conditions were more favorable to leniency. Among those who fled into the hills was Big John Aikman. He crossed over into adjoining Letcher County, where he performed a few well paid chores for one of the contending factions. Some time later the Governor sent troops into the mountains after him, and Big John, who was living with a half-brother, was brought back to Breathitt County for trial. He was sentenced to the penitentiary, but was pardoned after serving a short time. When Big John returned to Breathitt, he showed every sign of leading a peaceful life, but in a later feud he was unable to resist his customary role.

The election of a county judge to succeed Burnett and the regular county elections gave the Little-Burnett feud a somewhat futile, half-ironical ending. James Lindon became the new county judge. His wife was a sister of Edward Marcum, a lieutenant of the Union Army, and also a sister of James B. Marcum who figured in the worst of all the Breathitt feuds. Since Lindon had no blood ties in Breathitt, his sympathies were considered to be identical with those of his wife. This naturally kept feudal feelings alive. C. J. Little, the deputy sheriff who attempted to take his kinsman, Jason Little, into custody, was elected to succeed High Sheriff Hagins. This was a set-back to the adherents of Burnett and Hagins who, it is now evident, were genuinely seeking to strengthen the government of Breathitt County and take it out of the slough of feudalism.

Callahan-Strong Feud

The Callahan-Strong feud, which next stained the history of Breathitt with blood and hate, involved old family antagonisms, heated political rivalries, and economic competition. It was directed chiefly against the faction and influence of the aging Captain Bill Strong. There were others, chiefly James Deaton, who participated more directly and more dramatically than the old captain. The Strong faction, however, always represented one side of the contending powers in Breathitt. If "Uncle Bill," as Captain Strong became more affectionately known towards the end of the century, was not the power behind the throne, or else if he did not directly rule, as was seldom the case after the war, he was invariably the spearhead of the opposition. Like the other feuds, the Callahan-Strong feud originated in the bushwhacking days of the War between the States, and was the last to trace its beginning to some event during this period.

Ed Callahan, the leader of the Callahan faction, was the grandson of Wilson Callahan whom Captain Strong is traditionally said to have dispatched. Through skilful management and a dominating personality Ed amassed considerable wealth. He became captain of the Ku-Klux, which is said to have numbered over a thousand during its heyday in Breathitt. This was the same secret organization which rose to clandestine power in the South during the carpetbagging days. In the hands of Callahan it became a formidable weapon in the sparsely settled roadless hills of Breathitt. His warriors went about well-armed, many of them carrying two "Breathitt County pistols" apiece—a "Breathitt County pistol" being the biggest one that could be bought.

Ed Callahan was the most resourceful and in many respects one of the most imposing of the Breathitt feudists. While still a young man he was basking in the fullest splendor and glory that a well-heeled feudal chieftain could expect. Oftentimes, especially on Democratic convention days, he rode like a military commander into the county seat at the head of a procession of voters numbering anywhere from two to five hundred strong.

He supported his warrior crew by fairly extensive logging operations, principally in a disputed tract of timber on Bowling's Creek, a tributary of the Middle Fork. The timber was always taken to a certain clearing on the riverbank before being rafted and, when the tide came, carried down the river. While part of his men were busy in this phase of his logging business, others were busy hooking and "dehorning" the finest company logs afloat which Ed bought from them for small sums. These logs were then rebranded, and when the time came they went to the sawmills for which they were originally destined—rafted with the other (dehorned) logs! In this way the lumber companies bought some of their logs twice.

Callahan's home was some distance from the county seat, and in time it became something of a manor house for the inland domain over which he exercised a paternal rule, in the rustic style of a Scotch clan chieftain. As in days of feudal fealty, there were many young men who wished to make their homes with him and become his dependents. These youngsters would farm for him, and ordinarily they profited nicely from their labors, for the teams employed in logging required a great deal of feed.

Callahan's Rivalry with James Deaton

James Deaton, a rival in feudal fealties and in the logging business, was the peer of Callahan in physique, intelligence, and strength of character. They were neighbors, and both were flourishing mountain merchants. In personal and social matters, in political prestige and influence, as well as in business they were open competitors. They belonged to the same political party, the same church, and in other respects lived the same type of life. On convention days, Deaton, too, rode on a spirited mount at the head of a small army of voters who supported him in his opposition to the office-holding ambitions of the Callahan faction. It was on such occasions, at the head of his faithful followers, that Deaton seemed most lordly. His foes considered him relentless and revengeful, but others considered him kind and obliging. At times he was very arrogant and boastful. When in Jackson, with a superior force on his side, he oftentimes tantalized and upbraided young Callahan for no reason except that he liked to crow over his foe.

The Deatons, one of Breathitt's largest and most influential families, were divided, however, in their favors and friendship between James Deaton and Ed Callahan. For this reason there was no genuine Deaton-Callahan feud. Some of the Deatons looked upon Callahan as a scourge to Captain Strong who was also their enemy. It did not matter that during the bushwhacking days he was one of Strong's men. Even though Deaton and Strong had a mutual enemy, they did not become fellow conspirators, and James Deaton merely accepted but did not invite Strong's support in matters where the Callahan faction was concerned.

Callahan and Deaton soon found their interests treacherously antagonistic. Both cut prized timber from the same disputed lands, hauled it to the same riverbank where it was rafted on the same bar with dehorned logs, and it was then run to the same market where it netted a fat profit, and was often sold to the same buyers. They also hauled their merchandise from the same railroad station and over the same roads, freighted it in flat-bottomed boats along the same stream, and often sold it to the same customers. Both are also said at times to have stolen out on moonless nights, when the tide was promising, and cut the cable holding the timber of the other. Dark threats, known to be supported by plenty of ammunition, warded off the intruder who sought to save his timber. This made it necessary, particularly during the logging season, to keep a guard over the timber if it was not to fall into the possession of the other who would run it to market and pocket the proceeds. Such activities resulted in interminable litigation that continued many years after Deaton's death. It was partly as Deaton's attorney that J. B. Marcum incurred the dislike of Callahan, a dislike that later helped to bring about Marcum's death.

The End of the Deaton-Callahan Rivalry

The seemingly trivial disagreement that rang down the curtain on the rivalry of Callahan and Deaton was evidently planned. One day Callahan visited the sand bar where he and Deaton often rafted their own logs and dehorned those of others. He was accompanied by his men, among whom there were plenty of loaded firearms. Deaton and his men were busy rafting logs. Callahan stepped over to a canthook and picked it up. He claimed it as his own and announced his intention to take it with him. This so infuriated Deaton that he leaped for his Winchester.

The moment that Deaton picked up his rifle the Callahan group unloaded their shots on him. Deaton fell and died on the spot. The defendants involved in the shooting were indicted for murder, and each in turn testified that Deaton had threatened Callahan and was in the act of taking his life when his men shot Deaton to save Callahan's life. Deaton's men claimed that Callahan fired the first shot. Curiously enough, Bob Deaton, a first cousin of James Deaton, claimed that he fired the fatal shot. In the prosecution that followed, J. B. Marcum and his associates, as well as Captain Strong and his friends, were active in prosecuting Callahan. This fact stirred up the feudal spirit already existing between the Callahan and Strong forces, and a few years later it bore its bitter fruit.

It became evident during the first stages of the trial that the defense was not sufficiently strong to receive complete acquittal. It is related that Callahan was released from jail one night and, accompanied by a few of his friends, proceeded to contact the members of the jury, supposedly guarded in a boarding-house in Jackson. The husband of the lady of this house was one of the jurymen, and through his wife Callahan is said to have bought a favorable verdict. The majority of the jury were reputed to be "Ku-Kluxers" and therefore were holding out for an acquittal anyway. There were several others, three to be exact, who thought otherwise. Not until the money was actually produced, it is reported, did their opinion change, and then very quickly. The verdict of "not guilty" is said to have cost no more than $500.

The "Ku-Klux" Ride Five Hundred Strong

The most awesome event in the Strong-Callahan feud occurred some time after the killing of James Deaton. It was a night-hidden but impressive display of feudal justice and power. William Tharp, a highly respected citizen in his community, was marked for assassination—it is said with Strong's approval. His place in the pattern of this feud other than the events that follow is obscured. Strong's gunman, Hen Kilburn, had for months kept watch in numerous spots, but without bagging his game. Kilburn learned late one evening that Tharp was riding to Jackson the next morning by way of White Pine Creek, a fork of Cane Creek. He knew just the place for a comfortable ambush which he lost no time in preparing. "The Death of Many," the name given Kilburn's rifle, was loaded and ready for its next victim. That morning Tharp finally ambled along on his horse. "The Death of Many" barked out and Tharp fell dead from his mount. Tharp's body was found and the news spread to every part of the county in a short time. This time Strong's "firing-squad" had picked off an honored member of the powerful Klan. Kilburn, suspected and accused of the ambush, was arrested. After being placed in the Breathitt County Jail, young Callahan immediately sent out a war call to every part of the county. The word was "ten o'clock at night around the courthouse with arms." Every part of Breathitt promptly responded to the call that night. From north, south, east, and west men converged on Jackson, splashing through creek beds and cautiously picking their way over rocky paths. Jackson itself was quiet that night—quiet like a town where the whisper of death is heard. Only the whinnying of the horses, and the rustle of men's clothes, or the occasional squeak of leather revealed the avenging host. The townspeople who did not participate stayed inside when they saw or heard what was going on. Silent figures moved about the streets in a mysterious manner for awhile and then guards were posted at the entrances of all the dwellings in the town. A committee was selected to wait on the jailer, William Combs. They demanded the keys of the jail and were refused. Since the jailer was well and widely connected, a highly respected and honored citizen, he was not touched. The mob secured axes and hammers and proceeded to beat down the door of the jail. Kilburn was seriously wounded by an ax while the door was being broken down, but this seemed only to whet the fury of the mob.

 A Negro, thought to be guilty of no crime other than

BEGINNING BRANCH SCHOOL

carrying food to Kilburn in his many places of ambush, was jailed with him. Both were taken from the jail to the front door of the courthouse. A strong plea was made for the Negro's life, but the voice of a certain man is said to have bellowed forth his death sentence. Then, without further ceremonies, they were hanged. According to orders issued and posted on the courthouse door, their bodies were to remain suspended there between heaven and earth until eight o'clock the next morning. These orders were obeyed. The body of Kilburn, dangling before the door the next morning, was a gruesome and terrifying symbol for old Captain Strong. This hanging was seldom mentioned thereafter, for Callahan's power and the strength of the Klan had reached its peak. Their open enemies could find complete safety only in flight. The Ku-Klux returned home in safety and no one, as far as is known, was ever apprehended for the deeds of that night.

The Fall of Breathitt's Veteran Feud Chieftain

The Callahan-Strong feud waned as Callahan's power increased, but there was still one sweet morsel of revenge left—the now mellowed old man, Captain Strong, who had been stripped of his feudal prestige by the hanging of Kilburn. As "Uncle Bill" approached his dotage, he became less mindful of danger. Perhaps he wished during the twilight of his life to experience a feeling of greater freedom—to emancipate himself from fear and its continual watchfulness. At any rate he occasionally rode about on his game mule apparently unaware of any possible danger.

One morning the old captain was asked to go to the store, a trip of several miles. He saddled his mule and placed his little grandson behind him. At the store Uncle Bill made his purchases, talked awhile, and then started home. He was indeed a sad and forlorn figure. No longer could he muster a force strong and daring enough to take over the county courthouse! On his way back he traveled up Lick Branch, passing a low gap in the mountains. Here Big John Aikman, who since his release from prison had found the life of a feud gunman irresistible, had been waiting for some time with two boon comrades. When the old captain reached easy range, they fired on him from the dense evergreen woods. The first shot killed Strong and the next one the captain's faithful old mule. His grandson was apparently untouched, as the Breathitt feudists never harmed the children of their deadliest enemy. Big John and his accomplices ran out to the fallen body of the old chieftain and fired on him several times to make certain that he would never rise to fight again. The assassins then hid themselves in the woods until night when they stole away to report the success of their ambush.

Conclusion

The death of old Captain Strong brought to an inglorious end the last of the feuds directly originating in the bushwhacking days of the War between the States. The best-known of all the Breathitt vendettas, that bearing the names of Hargis, Cockrell, Marcum, and Callahan, concludes the feud history of the county. The often told tales and the much publicized events of this feud heaped upon Breathitt County a long-persisting infamy.

More recent difficulties, at Clayhole in 1921 and in Jackson in 1938 and 1940, have not assumed the proportions of a feud. Even though the county may have one or two well-broadcasted murders every year—for a killing in Breathitt always seems to be big news— educational facilities, better roads, in short, greater contact with modern forces have corroded the feudal spirit.

JACKSON TODAY

Jackson, seat of Breathitt County, straggles over the bottom lands and hillsides of the North Fork of the Kentucky River at the beginning of the famous Panbowl bend. Ranges of hills, rising abruptly like great fortifications on the west and more gently sloping on the east, surround it on every side. Two State highways that intersect here wind in long sweeps over steep hills or skirt rather narrow defiles along the riverbank before entering the town. On the far side of the North Fork, where it forms a quarter-circle as it begins to swing into the Panbowl bend, bluffs having the appearance of ancient fortifications scarred in immemorial battles, embolden the town's varied landscape.

In this picturesque setting Jackson has slowly grown from a wilderness settlement into a leisurely mountain community of a little over 2,000 people. It has passed through its boom period, sown its wild oats, and has now settled down to a quieter, more orderly development. As the commercial center of one of Kentucky's larger counties, Jackson presents a motley and democratic picture.

The corner of Main and Court streets unfolds an interesting cross section of life in Jackson in the earlier part of the morning. The courthouse, a chain grocery store, and the Breathitt County High School at the foot of the hill bring together a medley of young and old, of city folks and those "out in the county." High school boys and, to a lesser extent, high school girls while away ten or fifteen minutes before going to school. Farmers and their wives stand around to talk a bit before or after buying their groceries or going on "down" into town. The dignified, hard-working mountain woman, dressed in cotton, and more concerned with food and her children than the latest hat craze or the length of this year's dresses, may stop to exchange some pleasantry with a town cousin or a visiting relative turned out in metropolitan chic.

Around the dilapidated courthouse the overalled gentry and tenantry of the county gather to talk of their affairs, to exchange the latest local news, to review the political situation, and finally, to attend to whatever business, if any, they may have in town. On Saturdays, court days, during elections, and on other special occasions, when the weather permits, the town becomes a lively confusion of aimless milling about, of sociable "people-seeing," and incessant chatter. Trucks, jalopies, and new cars pull in at the curbs, load and unload, stay awhile and then pull out. "Taxi row," directly across from the courthouse, adds to the bustle of Courthouse Square. About a half dozen private cars used as taxis make fairly regular runs as far out into the country as fifteen or twenty miles.

There is no delivery of mail to Jackson homes and stores. For a brief spell in the early morning, and especially in the late afternoon after the train has arrived from Lexington, the post office becomes a magnet, drawing a small crowd from various parts of the town. The depot's waiting-room, opened only around the time of the two daily train arrivals, affords another slice of Jackson life. Students going home on week-ends, men working some place along the line, and other passengers coming to and going from Jackson add a bustling moment to the town's routine.

Jackson is primarily a town of people rather than of things and particular historic events. It has a definite and intimate personality that can only be fully savored by experiencing its many aspects. More important still, one must "learn" its people and be on their side. Blood ties and neighborliness count for much, and must be given their proper consideration. The town cannot be hurried, for it has retained much of the leisure of the countryside where time is measured by the rising and setting of the sun. It caters to no one as it still abides by the proud independence of the mountains. It is easygoing and sufficiently courteous to the stranger to be inquisitive and then become friendly.

Jackson is a town of electricity and natural gas, of two motion-picture theaters, of beauty shops, garages and filling stations, of ice cream sodas, and the radio. The

Louisville *Courier-Journal* and the *Lexington Herald* are read, and both have a comparatively large carrier circulation. Here, too, in the midst of hills where many old-fashioned ways still persist, the great all-American institutions flourish. Fads and gadgets found in Hoboken and San Francisco find their way here. The chief differences arise out of a vanishing past—of feuds, of quaint mountain characteristics and habits, of venerable folk beliefs, and of a speech savoring of the earth, the home hearth, and the personal ways of man.

Commercially, it is still a town of individual local proprietors. Only one nationally-known chain store, a grocery, has invaded the town. Jackson is the wholesale and retail center of the county and of a few adjoining communities in bordering counties, as well as the largest town between Winchester (*80 m. north*) and Hazard (*45 m. south*) on State 15.

Social life in Jackson, as in all communities where much of the gusto and many of the ways of the frontier still linger, is predominantly youthful. A junior college with approximately three hundred students, two high schools and a comparatively high birth-rate help perpetuate this characteristic. The center of this social life in Jackson is a drug store on Main Street. Here gather the young bucks and blades and the town's bevy of belles to sip soft drinks and spoon ice cream to the softened tunes of Tin-pan Alley's latest output. A dance floor and a phonograph in the back complete the picture.

Elsewhere, social and night life centers around restaurants and the other drug store in town. Jackson, like the county, is "wet." Dancing, if it is nothing more than a "hill-billy shuffle," is a popular form of entertainment in the few taverns along the hard-surfaced highway out of town. The ever-present nickelodeon indicates the mountaineer's high regard for music. If he favors the semi-melancholy type, as he is apt to do, it is because he has been musically nurtured on it and because it reflects something of his life.

Jackson also has that intimate social life that meets over the bridge table and carries out successfully such events of the year as President Roosevelt's Birthday Ball. The Junior and Senior proms are red-letter days since they are the only two occasions during the year when an outside orchestra is brought in. The School Fair, held the third Friday in October every year, is also a red-letter day. Hundreds of students and their teachers flock in holiday mood to Jackson. Several lodges, among them the Masons, Knights of Pythias, Daughters of America, and the Eastern Star vary the social routine of the town. Jackson's social life often takes on a distinctly community spirit. Softball, the event of the night in the summer, attracts between four and five hundred spectators. In the winter, basketball games, and occasionally amateur productions attract somewhat smaller but equally enthusiastic crowds. One of the most active organizations in Jackson, the Kiwanis Club, sponsors programs of every type. The work carried on by the Jackson Kiwanis is divided among several agencies in larger cities. As a reward for its active and varied service to the community, it was awarded first place among clubs of its size in the country at the national convention in San Francisco in 1938.

Jackson has many moods, for it is as changeable as the town's quiet but varied routine or the special incidents that punctuate this even flow. More so than in larger cities, it is sensitive to holidays and seasonal changes. It lives closer to the country, and because diversions are limited the people make more "to-do" about holidays. The stranger arriving on a pleasant Saturday morning when the many land contours, upon which Jackson is spread out, are bathed in sunshine will immediately conclude that the chief amusement is sitting and standing around to watch others sit and stand around. At other times, particularly after nine o'clock at night in winter weather, it is like a village that has been deserted, but with many windows and a few business places left lighted. An occasional straggler or two, perhaps a group on their way to one of the town's two drug stores, or its many restaurants, to its two pool parlors and its several liquor dispensaries, or to its motion-picture theaters tell the extent of night life in Jackson itself.

Hallowe'en is one of the more colorful occasions in the town. Young and old flock out, many of them wearing false faces and weird or bizarre dress. It is the time of "hants." Many people from "out in the county" come into town. For several hours that night the "main drag" is a continual shuffle. Banter flies back and forth. Some of the boys dress up as girls and some of the girls as boys. There is a great deal of horseplay, and a gay time results.

Christmas is celebrated in a typically American manner. Evergreen trees and decorations, Santa Claus and gifts, eggnog and fruit cake, and alcoholic beverages all combine to create the spirit of Yuletide. It is during Christmas rather than on the Fourth of July that firecrackers are set off. Safely up in the surrounding hills an occasional stick of dynamite is set off to give proper emphasis to a bit of celebrating. The sharp whir of rifle bullets and the spraying discharge of gunshot now and then echo through the valley.

Thanksgiving, New Year's, and Easter are also observed in a typically American manner. On Thanksgiving the turkey is rated king, although the day does not have quite as much importance as in other sections of the country. The New Year is always greeted with a salvo of gunfire.

Jackson, as all towns, has its distinguishing marks in people, sounds, and places. Familiar figures around town give it touches of somberness and romance. Some of them are vibrant with color, others drab with the graying of poverty and age. It also has the much cherished "inside" lore of the small town. Typical of these very human tidbits in the younger set was the confidential confession of the "lad" who plays good football for a high school in another county. In a moment of convivial holiday thoughtlessness he remarked that his team during the year had lost only those games in which he was unable to play because of a bad knee. Out of this incident has been fabricated a story replete with humor and personal tradition. Collectively, such stories form the very human basis for personal relationships and they weld together small towns into compact social units.

The descendants of some of Breathitt's notorious feudists, usually unknown as such, are familiar figures on Jackson's streets. One is surprised to find them a likeable, pleasant lot and just like "other people." Some of them are strikingly good looking and others are of ordinary homeliness. They are not at all like the dramatized newspaper accounts or the righteous book versions of inbred decadence.

The flow of water through the Panhandle Tunnel rises to a roar when the river is high, and fades into a soft whisper when it is low. It is the never-ending strain that insinuates itself into the life of Jackson. The whistle of southbound trains echoing and wailing as they chug through the "Cutoff" (see below), especially the long whistle of the afternoon train bringing in the mail, contributes a distinctive note in the diapason of sounds. The occasional blare of announcements over the public address system of a radio truck forms a welcome discordance. The bell in the courthouse tower is rung for the convening of the circuit court in the morning and the afternoon, and on other occasions, such as fires, public meetings, and on New Year's Day.

In its architecture and in the placement of homes and store buildings Jackson presents a curious variety. In this respect, as in most small towns, it is democratic. A ramshackle cottage may be only a door or so from a spacious home of modern appointments. A few of its houses have been left off the street lines. Many two-story homes situated on a hillside stand below street levels and from the front appear to be one-story. Jackson has many substantial homes of frame and brick construction. All but a couple of its older, frame-constructed store buildings are of brick. Sidewalk levels, especially down the steeper inclines, do not maintain the same grade as street levels. As a result some of its streets are high-curbed, and others below the street level are curbed inside.

The business section of Jackson is largely embraced in the area that begins at the courthouse and extends one block down the same street and then around the square. South Jackson has a scattering of business places in front of the depot, and it also has the town's only photographic studio. Unlike many of the Kentucky mountain towns, Jackson is not cramped.

South Jackson, strung out beneath steep hills on the opposite bottom of the North Fork, is connected with Jackson proper by an iron bridge. One of the town's two hotels, a large three-story frame building, is located here. The depot, a simple one-story red brick building, and other railroad structures are also situated here. The railroad dominates this part of the town and is the principal vein of life in this motley community. Frame houses, all but

BREATHITT HIGH'S HONOR DRAMATIC GROUP—1939

a few of them needing paint and half of them dilapidated, extend south for about two miles along the ever-widening table of the long-curving North Fork.

On the outskirts of Jackson along State 15, particularly its southern exit, small wooden houses are strung out along both sides of the highway. The more numerous ones on the riverside often sit half way below the roadside level, so that one can look down on their porches, or on to their roofs. All but a few of them are wooden, usually of straight boards and planks, most of them unpainted or badly needing a new coat of paint, and some of them so ramshackle that it seems a puff of wind could demolish them. A few here and there are crazily tilted to one side. Below them, on the narrow strips of bottom land, are patches of corn, and close by are askewed sheds for stock and fodder, and less frequently a pigsty and a corncrib. Chickens peck around in the small barnyards. The people who live along here till their corn patches and their small gardens, and occasionally work for more prosperous farmers and at odd jobs. Many of them, when all of these meager opportunities fail, get Work Relief jobs. Yet, like true mountaineers, these people have a stoical attitude. They are still pioneers inured to the hardships of life, having their fun where they find it, working to keep alive, sometimes eating as well and even better than most city folks. They have kept their sense of humor in the face of privations that would have defeated and crushed a less sturdy breed. They are seldom ambitious and as seldom shiftless.

THE HISTORY OF JACKSON

When the commissioners appointed by the legislature to locate the county seat changed it from Quicksand to Jackson, there was only a twelve-acre field and a log cabin on the new site. The balance of Simon Cockrell's tract, including all the bottom part, was covered with native forest trees, many of them very large. Mr. Cockrell conveyed to the county as a gift ten acres which is now the original town site. He then sold the remainder of the surrounding land, containing several hundred acres, for $1,000. Land in the mountain country was very cheap at that time, and Cockrell had previously tried to sell this tract for $500 without success. John Hargis, who purchased it, had emigrated from Pikeville on the Big Sandy, where nine of his ten children were born. He was the first man to move into Breathitt Town, where he bought two lots on Main Street. He erected on them four or five log cabins which were used for a time as hostels.

The ten-acre town site was subdivided into lots which were sold to the highest bidder. J. Green Trimble attended the auction of these lots and purchased two, one in the western end of the town for $37, and another one for $60. Jerry South purchased a corner lot for $75 and built a two-story log house which was used as a hotel and called "Our House." Isaac Back bought the lot opposite the Courthouse Square, upon which the John Hargis Building nows stands, for $30. Jackson's first merchant, Thomas Sewell, of Harlan Courthouse, purchased two lots west of the courthouse, and erected upon them a dwelling and storehouse of hewed logs. On Christmas Day, 1840, his family arrived in Jackson, on horses and mules, from Harlan County. Accompanying his wife, their daughter, Fanny, and their two sons, William and Benjamin, were two young laborers, Bill Wright and Jordon Gross. Mr. Sewell was a successful merchant and continued to live in Jackson until the outbreak of the War between the States, when he moved to Irvine, Estill County. J. Green Trimble commenced selling goods for him at Jackson about March 1, 1841. Thomas J. Frazier, the second merchant to open a store in Jackson, also represented Breathitt County in the State Legislature.

Among the other early settlers of Jackson were John Sewell, uncle of Thomas Sewell the merchant, John Cardwell, Dr. Parsons, a local Methodist preacher, Alexander Patrick, Jerry South, Rev. Nixon Covey, William Davis, and two brothers from the East, James B. and William Griffing. These last two were gentlemen of education and considerable business ability who thought that the county in its undeveloped state offered opportunities for accumulating considerable money. When their anticipations did not materialize, after about three years' residence in Jackson, they moved to Memphis, Tennessee, where they engaged in a successful lumber business.

In the spring of 1841, a little over a year after the county seat was located at this point, Mr. Trimble "spent one day at hard work, assisting in rolling logs, which were burned on the ground in the bottom below, in the bend of the river adjoining where the bridge is now located." (*Recollections*, p. 10.) This was also the first year that corn was planted on this part of the farm.

The county seat, as was then sometimes the custom, was first known as Breathitt Town. In 1845 the name was changed to Jackson by an act of the State Legislature in memory of the old hero of the Battle of New Orleans, Gen. Andrew Jackson, who eight years before had completed his second term as seventh President of the United States. Among the early acts of the Kentucky General Assembly relating to Jackson was one in 1841 providing for an additional constable for the town. The following year this constabulary district was extended two miles from "the town of Breathitt." In an 1845 act the trustees of Jackson, Jeremiah W. South, Thomas Hagins (*sic*), Simon Bohanon, Jesse Spurlock, and John Hays were authorized to change an alleyway for John Hargis.

For about a decade after its establishment as the county seat, Jackson grew in a modest way. It had the usual hopes of a new town with all kinds of possibilities. It soon settled back, however, to the rather humdrum existence of an insignificant and isolated village in the Kentucky Mountains. Its small population fluctuated widely. Three or four families, either by taking up residence or moving away, increased or decreased the number of its citizens from 50 to 100 per cent. A stranger passing through was an important event.

The War between the States

In the early 1860's Jackson still had only a few houses. Its two stores, houses, jail, courthouse, and post office were all built of logs. On the hill now known as Yo Hill there was one cabin. It was not until after the War between the States that "Old" Bill Combs built two plank homes, the first in the history of Jackson. The streets resembled the narrow, mudhole roads common all over the county until a few years ago. There were not many horses, and only about three wagons in Breathitt County. Most of the hauling, outside of navigable streams, was done by a two-wheel cart and a yoke of oxen. Dry goods, groceries, and other products were all brought to Jackson in boats. Beef tallow candles were used for lighting. There was still no church, but a preacher would occasionally come to Jackson and hold services in some home. Around this time there was one doctor in Jackson, and sometimes another doctor from an adjoining county would come and stay awhile.

Capt. W. L. Hurst in one of his reminiscences recalled that on his first visit to Jackson after the war he found the town almost depopulated and business of all kinds entirely suspended. The grass on Main Street had grown up until it was waist-high in places, and almost the only signs of the street left were little paths running here and there through the tall grass. While here on this trip he and some friends ran a gray squirrel up a tree in the heart of town, and had fine sport shooting at him with revolvers. The population of the town in 1870 as given in Collins' *History of Kentucky* was fifty-four.

In 1866 Breathitt's first brick courthouse, replacing one of logs, was built. It was a small two-story building with the courtroom on the first and three jury rooms on the second floor. The offices of the county and circuit court clerks were housed in a two-room brick building, located on the site of the present well or close by. This building was burned sometime after midnight in 1873. It was widely believed that fire was set to this building in order to destroy certain deeds. The only document saved from the fire was the first circuit court order book which covered the years 1839-49. Shortly after the building was burned and its documents destroyed by fire, numerous forged deeds appeared.

During the War between the States, Jackson often became the rendezvous of the guerrilla bands whose depredations started the county feuds. It became the feud capital of "Bloody Breathitt." Law and order was usually that imposed by the strongest, most unscrupulous faction in the county.

Before the Coming of the Railroad

Other events and circumstances, more cheerful and promising, marked the growth of Jackson during the last quarter of the nineteenth century. Two decades before the Kentucky Union (Lexington & Eastern) reached Jackson, the railroad fever had touched Breathitt and raised the temperature of commercial hopes. In 1873 the State Legislature approved a tax of ten cents on each hundred dollars assessed for the purpose of having a survey made through Breathitt County for a railroad. Between 1884-86 Clay City, in the Red River Valley of Powell County, was connected with the Chesapeake & Ohio route to Lexington by a line fourteen miles long. The ups-and-downs of early railroad politics and finances kept Jackson in a state of anticipation for many years. The town changed little. Several important additions to the physical appearance of Jackson were made around 1887. Jackson Academy (Lees College) and the present courthouse were built during the year. During the decade an imposing brick residence was built by Charles J. Little, a leading merchant of the town (*see Points of Interest in Jackson*). A Methodist congregation, organized by Rev. J. J. Dickey, erected a small frame church building.

A letter written to the editor of *The Jackson Times* (Dec. 10, 1924) gives a sketch of the town and an inkling of its life in the early eighties:

I lived in Jackson thirteen years, from 1882 to 1895. One who did not know Breathitt County at that time cannot have any just conception of the improvement. Then there were only eighteen residences in Jackson . . . The only business that brought money into the county was logging . . . There was no newspaper in the county then, not until about 1890. Jackson was fifty miles from any railroad. The daily mail was our greatest asset, and it required three days for a letter or paper to come from Lexington and Louisville, and two days to come from the nearest railroad.

The morning dailies reached us on the evening of the third day after they were printed. All freight was hauled fifty miles at $1.00 per hundred . . .

Boarding in Jackson was $2.00 per week; everything furnished except laundry. The courthouse was a one-room structure, with three jury rooms upstairs, and the clerks' offices were both in a small brick building in the courthouse yard . . .

Near the end of the legislative session in 1890, perhaps in anticipation of the entrance of the railroad, Jackson was incorporated. Its boundaries as defined in the act began at the mouth of the Bridge Branch, above (that is south of) the town of Jackson, then up this branch with its meanderings to a large sycamore tree, and just above a coal chute. It then continued in a straight line across the hill to the river, at the mouth of a drain just above an old schoolhouse, and including the schoolhouse and grounds. From here it extended up the river to a point opposite the upper end of a field belonging to J. S. Hargis, crossed the river and the Panhandle and continued down the river with its meanders to the mouth of the Cutoff Branch. It then continued up this branch to the top of the gap, along the road in a straight line down to and across the river, and up the river to the place of beginning. Within these corporate limits there were around four hundred acres and approximately four hundred people, according to *The Jackson Hustler*.

Between 1888 and 1890 the Kentucky Union Railroad Company extended its line up the valley of Red River from Clay City across the North Fork at the mouth of Middle Fork and then to Elkatawa, only a few miles from Jackson. There was great expectancy in Jackson during this period. John Goff, Jr., of Indian Fields, Clark County, established *The Jackson Hustler* on December 28, 1888. The first equipment consisted of a seven-column Army press which was placed in a room in the courthouse. The first issue, of which three hundred copies were printed, was set up by a Mr. Rowland, then a seventeen-year-old lad from Richmond. Mr. Goff announced that Breathitt had entered the ranks of progressive counties and proposed to keep step with the advancing columns. He immediately began to advertise the wonderful resources of what he christened the Promised Land. On July 3, 1890, Rev. J. J. Dickey took charge of the paper.

The Jackson Hustler, in its issue of March 6, 1891, gave a brief sketch of the town for a number of persons who had never seen Jackson and to whom copies of that particular issue were sent. Among the residences were a number of first-rate dwellings. The public buildings were the present courthouse, then considered "a large new brick courthouse, with modern conveniences," a two-story brick Academy Building, large enough to accommodate 250 pupils, and worth with its three acres of land, $10,000. A beautiful church thirty by 45, recently erected by the Presbyterians was then the only house of religious worship. There were seven storehouses and two more in process of construction, a sawmill, a cornmill, and a flourmill that was not running then. The Kentucky Union Railroad was graded to the opposite side of the river.

The Railroad Arrives and the Boom Is On

The railroad, after many delays, finally reached Jackson on July 15, 1891. The town, after this, became a frontier terminus. It was the point from which supplies for a half dozen mountain counties were distributed and at which all the mountain products were gathered for shipment. Among the innumerable advantages that the railroad opened up for the mountain people of this section were occasional excursions. On the first of August, 1894, the Kentucky Union Railroad Company sold round trip tickets from Jackson via Lexington to Niagara Falls for $10.85. The rate to Toronto and Put-in-Bay was $1.00 extra, and to Thousand Islands $5.00.

Eighteen hundred and ninety-one was, quite naturally, a year of much building activity. Brickmaking was in full blast again, reminding the editor of *The Hustler* of 1886-87 when so many brick were burned in Jackson. George Rice was preparing his yard for the manufacture of brick, and J. W. Cardwell was preparing to burn 200,000 brick in the first kiln in order to build the business house, the foundation of which he laid in the fall of 1890. William D. Back was having lumber cut to build a hotel on the lot which he had recently bought from J. M. Snowden.

The town itself was also making civic improvements during this year. Some of the merchants were putting up street lamps in front of their stores. Editor J. J. Dickey exhorted them not to let the good work stop until the whole town was "illuminated." Capt. N. B. Combs and his force of men were laying sidewalks on Main Street and on Broadway. Rights-of-way were given for the newly proposed Academy (College) Street. When it was not properly opened by the folks along the way, *The Hustler* remarked: "It will soon be time to make gardens and then it will be too late."

In the line of business a visiting blacksmith, W. E. Ryland, of Johnson County, was working at the shop of Herman Centers "ready to do all things of blacksmithing and woodwork. He could make anything from a shovel plow to a buggy." A new millinery and dressmaking shop, Combs, Hagins and Patrick, was established in Jackson with a large new stock of spring and summer goods in the latest and most fashionable styles. The Lexington Steam Laundry had an agent in the town who gathered up shirts, collars and cuffs, which were sent to Lexington to be done up.

Jackson was even making strides in musical culture during this period of lush commercial activities. It could boast of thirteen organs, three pianos, and a group of singers in 1891. A piano company installed one of their instruments at the Riverside Hotel where Miss Katie Patrick brought out "its power and pathos with her magic touch." Three years later, when Mr. Charles J. Little purchased one, the town had nine pianos and twenty organs, an average of one to every white family. During the same year Mr. J. E. Patrick was mentioned in the local press for purchasing a twelve-volume leather-bound set of the *Encyclopedia Britannica* for $27.

In the 1890's there was much agitation for better roads in the county and for better mail service. John Goff mailed a letter at Jackson to the Clark County National Bank, Winchester, on the fifth or sixth of March,

LOST CREEK CONSOLIDATED SCHOOL

1891, which did not reach its destination until the eighteenth of March. No mail left the town from the sixth to the fifteenth on account of landslides.

Jackson was a "rip-snorting" town for about two decades after the railroad reached it. It had the virility of a boom town on a frontier. It was free, uncouth, unashamed, and ambitious. Nearly every man went around armed, as was then the custom. On Christmas Eve all the stores closed at four o'clock in the afternoon because the shooting started in earnest about that time. It wasn't long until the thin, blue haze from frequent gunfire hung like a light fog over the town.

An undated clipping from the Jackson newspaper headed "The New Jackson" recalls these earlier Christmases:

> The Christmas just past was the most quiet ever seen in Jackson. There was no disorder during the entire week, not even a case of drunkenness during the whole time. Xmas tree celebrations were held at all the churches and everybody seemed to have a good time and everyone felt absolutely secure in going anywhere on the streets, either at night or day. We have seen the time when this could not be done and the time when it seemed worth a man's life to attend to his regular business during a part of the holidays.
>
> We are glad that these troublous times are over and order is now restored and everybody seems to be happy. There are very few of those responsible for the former troubles here now . . .

Around 1905 a drummer, checking in at the old Hotel Arlington overlooking the river, would have been asked by the clerk whether he wanted a room with or without electricity. In the morning he possibly would have sat down for breakfast at one of the large tables, each capable of seating a dozen or more guests in the hotel dining-room. Among the gentlemen already eating was one who more than likely picked up the massive sugar bowl and poured sugar into his cup of coffee until it overflowed. This same gentleman would then reach down for his .45 calibre and proceed to stir his coffee with the muzzle end.

Breathitt's First and Only Legal Hanging

On the afternoon of Friday, June 28, 1895, the first and only legal hanging that has ever taken place in Breathitt County was held in Jackson's Courthouse Square. On this day, at 1:53 P.M., "Bad" Tom Smith, mountain desperado of French-Eversole feud fame, was hanged for the murder of Dr. J. E. Rader, of Jackson.

As a young boy of fourteen Tom Smith was first attacked by fits which increased in severity as he became older. Early in the night, soon after he went to sleep, his whole frame was shaken, and he made a noise that could easily be heard three hundred yards away. They lasted only a few moments, but were terribly severe. When they were over he spat out blood freely. On the night of February 5, 1895, Dr. Rader was invited out to Mrs. Catharine McQuinn's, Tom's forty-eight-year-old paramour, ostensibly to watch his convulsions when they occurred. "Bad" Tom had drunk such quantities of liquor, however, that medical treatment was impossible. Since widow McQuinn lived four miles from Jackson, Dr. Rader stayed all night, and the three of them occupied the same room. During the night, Tom Smith raised up out of his drunken stupor and shot Dr. Rader while he was asleep.

At seven-thirty on the morning Tom Smith was to die, High Sheriff Breck Combs took Tom Smith to the river where he was baptized. The hanging was scheduled for 11:00 A.M. when Deputy Sheriff William Bryant announced to the large crowd assembled that it had been postponed until 1:00 P.M. Services were conducted up until and after this time. On the scafford, erected near the jail, Tom Smith confessed that he killed Dr. Rader and several other men, either by himself or with an ally.

He then stepped back from the edge of the scaffold where he had been standing, a curtain was drawn around him and a black hood placed over his head. The hang-knot was next slipped around his neck. While this morbid ritual was going on "Bad" Tom, who knew Sheriff Combs personally, remarked "you're doing something to me, Breck, I could never do to you." Among the other last words that he spoke was the exhortation to "beware of whiskey and bad women." As the high sheriff was taking up the ax to cut the rope that released the trigger of the trap door, Smith cried out in a loud voice: "Lord have mercy on me."

Many women were in the large crowd that turned out to see this gruesome sight. Some of them fainted and others cried. Men and women alike turned their backs. A heavy, death-like silence hung over the scene. After about fifteen minutes the dangling body was pronounced dead, taken from the scaffold and placed in the coffin that awaited nearby.

Jackson at the End of the Century

The 1890's brought not only the excitement of the railroad and the sensationalism of a public hanging to Jackson, but numerous and much needed improvements. Several churches were organized on a solid foundation, a bridge was built across the North Fork, and a bank was incorporated. The Breathitt County Citizens Bank began business on February 2, 1891. The safe, hauled from the terminus of the railroad, was "both fire and burglar proof with the best time lock on it that is made." Several other banks have played a part in the commercial life of Breathitt. The Jackson Deposit Bank was founded around 1900. The First National Bank, the only one still operating, was established about a decade later. The Hargis Commercial Bank, opened around 1912, had a somewhat spectacular death in the depression, for it is said that more than half of Breathitt County "went busted" with it.

Until 1899 a ferryboat was used to cross the North Fork at Jackson in high water; in low water, logs that were nailed together served as a crossing. The first bridge, removed in 1908 to Lost Creek where it was erected across Troublesome Creek, was a tollbridge. Candies, fruits, and other confections were sold at the tollhouse. This bridge was leased to the highest bidder every year by the Breathitt Fiscal Court. The first bid was let on the third of January, 1899, at $1,300.

The second and present bridge at Jackson was completed in 1908 at a cost of approximately ten thousand dollars. It was brought in from "old" Virginia and considerably widened, as it had been a railroad bridge. The bridge is 372 feet long and 28 feet wide. Like the first bridge, it was built by Breathitt County and leased as a tollbridge to the highest bidder every year. No tolls were collected on Sunday. Mr. Roscoe C. Back, commonwealth's attorney (1940), remembers that when bridge tolls were collected boys played under the bridge and sometimes found pennies that were dropped by the collector.

Probably the oldest business building still standing

in Jackson is the A. D. Crawford Store, a two-story frame building, built around 1895. The building, now somewhat warped and dilapidated, is used today (1940) as a hardware storeroom. The oldest brick building still standing, the Day Brothers Store, was built in the late 1890's.

Two men who, by their integrity and devotion to civic ideals, helped shape the history of Jackson and Breathitt County during this period were David B. Redwine and O. H. Pollard. Mr. Redwine, of Magoffin County birth, came to Jackson as a young man about the time the railroad reached the town. Before coming to Breathitt he had taught school a couple of years in Elliott County. His only possessions when he arrived in Jackson, other than the clothes he wore, were a red bandana handkerchief and an extra pair of socks. After reading law, he was admitted to the bar and was elected circuit judge around 1900. He served in that capacity until his death in 1913. O. H. Pollard, who came to Jackson around 1900, was also a lawyer. He was later appointed attorney for the L. & N. R. R., a position he held until his death. Mr. Pollard, respected and beloved by all citizens, was an outstanding figure in church, school, and other civic affairs.

Marcum's Assassination

One of the bloodiest pages in the history of Jackson and Breathitt County during the first decade of the twentieth century was the assassination of U. S. Commissioner J. B. Marcum, on May 4, 1903. Immediately after this the town entered a period of dark terror. There was fear among all those who had in the smallest way displeased the clique then in power. Shortly afterwards there was published in the newspaper a lengthy accusation against the slain man, declaring, in effect at least, that the killing was a good and deserved deed. A partial exodus from Jackson took place. Many of Marcum's relatives, the Cockrells who were allied to the Marcums, and numerous sympathizers sought refuge at distant or hidden places. At night the streets were almost totally deserted, and only those sure of protection ventured forth. Churches were vacant and for many months services were suspended altogether. Suspicion and fears were rampant. The town was in the grip of a seemingly merciless tyrant. No one dared to speak of the matter openly, and even in private—in family circles and among close friends — remarks were guardedly made, if they were made at all. Finally, when the Governor sent in the State Militia, a normal flow of life was resumed.

Development After 1905

Less sensational events that filled in the even-tempered, work-a-day life of Jackson partially obscured the infamies of 1903. During the next two decades the town began to assume a more permanent physical appearance. A brick grade school and then later a separate high school building were erected.

The present-day depot, begun in 1910, was finished the following year at a cost of approximately $13,000. The first depot was the wooden structure now used for freight. A boxcar was used as the first telegraph office.

The (Missionary) Baptist Church, organized in the late 1890's with fourteen charter members, erected a new brick building at the corner of Main and Broadway in 1915-16. The Guerrant Memorial Presbyterian Church, a gray stone building, replaced the frame building which was destroyed along with the Baptist Church in the Halloween fire of 1913. The first Presbyterian congregation in Jackson was organized in the 1880's by Dr. E. O. Guerrant to whom the present church is a memorial. The present Methodist Church was built in 1922. It also replaced an earlier church which was dedicated in July, 1894, by Rev. T. W. Barker, of Falmouth. The Christian Church, organized in 1904, erected their first church building in 1906, and in 1924 a more imposing building was completed at a cost of $63,000.

Only two of Jackson's dozen or more hotels still exist. The Jefferson, on Main Street, was built in 1913, and the Ewen, in South Jackson, was built around 1905. Other hotels, most of them little more than boarding-houses that have figured in the history of the town, include the Stacy, Marcum, Arlington, Riverside, Thompson, Crain, Haddix, Back, Combs, Stidham, and Patrick.

The first semblance of motion-picture entertainment was the magic-lantern theater opened around 1906 by Lick Whitaker in the old Armour Building. It was known as the Hippodrome and had a seating capacity of approximately three hundred. Children were charged ten cents and adults fifteen cents. The "flicker" movies soon took the place of the "slide movies," and then the "talkies" reached Jackson not long after they had been established in large cities.

The most spectacular and destructive fire in Jackson's history occurred on Halloween night, 1913, interrupting an evening of costumed celebrating and convivality. Thirty-six buildings were burned including the Baptist and Presbyterian churches, a hotel, drug store, and the post office. The damage, amounting to about $35,000, was insured for only $1,500 which was divided between the two churches. The fire started on Broadway when an oil stove exploded in the home of R. A. Hurst. It then spread north and south on both sides of the street, reaching Main Street on both sides and continuing on out Broadway. The fire which spread rapidly in leaping, crackling flames was fought untiringly and heroically by a bucket brigade for about four hours. From all parts of Jackson and its environs men answered the alarm which was given by an almost incessant shooting of guns. Blankets and quilts were soaked in water and then thrown on other buildings to keep them from catching fire. While the hotel was burning a man was seen throwing furniture and mirrors out the windows and later he was seen struggling down the stairs with a feather bed on his back. After the fire downtown Jackson presented a picture of makeshift businesses. Barbershops were set up on the sidewalk, and customers were trimmed and shaved in the open air and in public view.

Jackson's more modern construction dates from this fire. Materials were selected along more fireproof lines to prevent a reoccurrence of the Halloween fire. Several brick buildings that added greatly to the appearance of the town were erected after this, among them the three-story Federal Building in 1916.

Two Decades at the End of a Century as County Seat

Three of the most outstanding landmarks added to Jackson in the twenties were the Bach Memorial Hospital, the three-story dormitory building of Lees College, and a modern city high school building. During the decade of the "thrilling thirties" a modern county high school building and a colonial style county jail were erected. Through aid of the Federal Work Relief program, which made these possible, a large community playground and stadium were built (*see Points of Interest in Jackson*). New and improved streets were also made possible through this program. Other less tangible contributions to the life of Jackson and Breathitt County were also made by this program, including varied recreational opportunities. A county library was opened in Jackson in 1930, the first public library in Breathitt County. A swinging bridge was erected across the North Fork from the foot of Court Street to the Panhandle. An airport laid out on the outskirts of South Jackson gave the town an emergency landing field.

The modernization of Jackson as far as utilities were concerned took place slowly. A portable electric plant first supplied electricity around 1902. Service was irregular and uncertain for many years. Today Jackson is served by the Kentucky and West Virginia Power and Light Company which covers a large part of eastern Kentucky. The city water system, which gets its supply from the North Fork, has been in operation since 1929. A sewerage system was installed at this time, too. Natural gas was first piped into the city during the latter part of 1936. Many homes in Jackson still get their water from the wells which are occasionally seen along the town's streets. The first semaphore or light signal was installed in November, 1937, at the intersection of College Avenue and Broadway.

Jackson, like a hundred other towns of its size in Kentucky, started as a settlement in the wilderness. Through a defective land title it became a county seat, and then for a half century it was an insignificant hamlet in the rugged fastness of the Kentucky foothills. After the War between the States it gradually became known as the feud capital of "Bloody Breathitt." The railroad brought it prosperity and in a year turned it from a sleepy village into a bustling railroad terminus. Strong-willed men, who thought little of stooping to the most desperate Machiavellian tactics, struggled to control the county seat as well as the county. Not until the railroad was extended to

Hazard, in 1912, did the intense struggle for political power and attendant financial considerations relax. Even then there was a strong tradition and many bloody events of the past still live in memory, and some still live in more tangible form. Today Jackson has become an easy-going, peaceful town. There is nothing to suggest its oftentimes hectic past—the intoxication of yesterday is gone. It has settled down, in keeping with its size, to the uneventful but wise task of "cultivating its garden."

BREATHITT COUNTY COURTHOUSE

"BOOK-LARNIN'" TO EDUCATION

The first schools in Breathitt were subscription schools, so called because they were maintained by tuition fees or "subscriptions." They were sometimes started by a single individual, an enterprising farmer with a numerous offspring, or the young man of dubious education "knocking about" the country. The teacher was occasionally a community character, either supplementing his regular work or else not much account at anything else according to frontier values but "school-keeping." In almost every case educational preparation was extremely low and even nonexistent. A few, perhaps, made up for their lack of knowledge by their enthusiasm.

J. Green Trimble, one of the earliest merchants of the county, attended a subscription school taught by William Cockrell who, in addition to his school teaching, farmed, surveyed, and preached. In Mr. Trimble's *Recollections of Breathitt* (p. 15), he gives an authentic and colorful picture of this school which he attended for all of sixty days during 1837 or thereabouts:

> Mr. Cockrell drew up an agreement which was signed by himself and his patrons, binding himself to teach spelling, reading, writing and arithmetic to the best of h[i]s knowledge for the term of one quarter (three months,) for which the patrons were to pay him $2.00 tuition and he was to board among the scholars. The only books we used were the Webster's blue back speller, New York Reader and Pikes Arithmetic, in the last of which one-half or more of the problems were in English money—pounds, shillings and pence. We were permitted to study, read and spell aloud, and each of the pupils tried to excel his neighbor in the loud tones of his voice. In learning the spelling lesson of fifteen minutes on Friday evening the class could be heard a half a mile.

These schools were sometimes called "frog schools" because the pupils made a sound like little frogs when they were studying. The teacher was often paid in furs, foods, and other products raised or manufactured in the community. More than one schoolmaster accepted corn liquor, which sold for fifty cents per gallon, as part pay on his salary, according to Mr. Granville Pearl Noble.

The "little red schoolhouse" of American lore was something of a palace compared with the early schoolhouses of Breathitt. They were one-room buildings of the most primitive and haphazard construction. Various kinds of logs, hewn and unhewn, were used usually before they were seasoned. In winter and summer alike breezes circulated through the half-chinked cracks, and with a little squeezing the smallest children could crawl out of the building. An occasional schoolhouse was floored with puncheons, but a flooring of bare earth was almost as common as bare feet. The roof was covered either with boards or "shakes." If there was a window or windows they were covered with greased paper, sometimes protected with crude shutters or more frequently not at all. More elegantly built schoolhouses had "stack" chimneys of mud, sticks, and stones which vented both heat and smoke. On cold days roaring log fires in mammoth fireplaces provided the only cheerful and comfortable note as well as the only artificial lighting in this early schoolhouse.

When Mr. Trimble was one of William Cockrell's pupils, the schoolhouse then in use:

> ... was built of round logs, about 20 feet square, covered with four-foot boards laid on ribs instead of rafters, upon which were placed upright poles to keep them in position instead of nailing. The floor was made of poplar puncheons about ten feet long, hewed with a broad-ax to the thickness of about three inches. There were no windows. As a substitute for writing tables there was a poplar log the length of the room and two feet in diameter, and split in two and dressed. One-half of it formed one of the logs of the house and was placed about four feet from the floor, and the other half was used as a seat at the writing table. The log extended considerable into the room, leaving a large open space above it for light. In this space was placed a rough frame covered with white paper, which was saturated with lard to make it transparent and was a substitute for glass, which had not yet been introduced into that country at the time. The furniture of the schoolhouse consisted of one chair, which was occupied by the school master (as he was called), a black hickory stick about four feet long, which stood in the corner by the school master (and which was used at times with great severity) and a small wooden paddle which hung on a nail, and which was used on the hands of the smaller children for minor offenses. There was also a block thirty inches high in the middle of the floor, and known as the Dunce Block, upon which were placed

those who were deficient in their lessons or were guilty of minor misdemeanors. The seats in the schoolhouse consisted of four wooden benches without backs, and a sufficient number of fence rails to accommodate the balance of the scholars. [*Ibid., pp.* 15-16.]

Another subscription school that performed yeoman service for a decade or more was established by Henry Combs on a portion of his farm at Clayhole. Henry, one of the five sons of Harrison Combs by his first wife, became one of the most prosperous farmers in Breathitt, took three wives and sired fourteen children by the first two and none by the third. For his numerous progeny and the children of neighbors he erected a one-room schoolhouse of hewed poplar logs chinked with mud. His own children walked one and one-half miles over a small mountain to attend this school. There were no windows in the structure, and the only two openings were for a door and one in the rear presumably for a fireplace that was never used. The bare ground served as a floor. The only equipment consisted of benches made by halving medium size logs and smoothing the split sides. Two holes were then burned or bored in each end of the bark side, and pegs were whittled to fit securely into these. The legs were spread out to afford greater support—since the master in the person of George Chapman, brought in from Virginia, had to sit with his pupils on the smoothed surface of these split logs.

The teacher had no desk, and consequently had to use his lap for the little writing that was done. Goose-quill pens and ink made from pokeberries were used by teacher and pupils alike at that time. The school term in the Combs school extended through the customary three months, but beginning around the first of September instead of August, and lasting until the end of November.

When the weather became severely cold, and there was no fireplace, the room was heated by a log fire built in the center of the room on the dirt floor. In a room, sometimes smoke-filled, where the principal light came from the crackling blazes of a log fire, the task of learning to read, spell, and "do sums" could not have seemed very important or been very inviting. Yet these subscription schools, conducted by men whose zeal for imparting knowledge disregarded many adverse conditions, fulfilled an invaluable service. The fundamentals of education which they offered laid the foundation for a more widespread and public system of education. The thin leaven of learning in Breathitt County, which they sustained for several decades, was barely sufficient for the functions of law and government. Not many of the teachers and preachers of this period had the benefit of more than a ninety-day education; and with that they felt equal to the task of teaching others.

Another early school was located on Quicksand at the place now called the Mouth of Loveless Branch, around 1865. This school, as remembered by Mr. Miles Bach, of Quicksand, who was ninety-six years old in 1939, was taught by Hiram Hagins, a brother of former Sheriff John L. Hagins. Like all the other schoolhouses, this was a log building with a dirt floor and split boards for a door. The term began in August and extended through October. During 1870 a school was opened in the church house at the Mouth of South Fork of Quicksand Creek, and about this time the Round Bottom community on Quicksand Creek built a schoolhouse of beech logs with an earthen floor, board roof, one door, and no chimney.

In several places "meeting-houses" were used as schools. A deed of property on Turkey Creek and Beginning Branch, recorded in 1858, and re-recorded in 1874 after the burning of county records in 1873, refers to a lot on which a meeting-house used as a schoolhouse stood. The lot was exempted from taxation as long as it was used for religious or educational purposes, but was to revert to the heirs of Curtiss Jett if unused for a period of twelve months. This was a subscription school opened by Curtiss Jett, a prosperous, slave-owning landholder along the Middle Fork. It was located near his home, about one and one-half miles from the Mouth of Turkey Creek at its confluence with the Middle Fork. Mr. Jett employed private teachers to instruct his eleven children, those of his relatives, and possibly those of neighboring families who were able and willing to pay a fee for their schooling. Miss Anna Searcy, from Madison County, near Richmond, one of the teachers employed by Curtiss Jett, married one of his sons, Stephen, Jr., who was several years her junior. When the last of Curtiss Jett's children had "passed through" this school, it was discontinued, and according to the terms of the deed reverted to the estate and was again taxed. The Jett school was attended by former State Senator A. H. Hargis, around 1870.

Other mentions of early schools are found in county court orders for renewing roads. At the October term, in 1873, the county court ordered the review of a road "near Herald's on the Middle Fork and its tributaries from the mouth of Puncheon Camp Creek to the schoolhouse just below the Mouth of Old Buck, on both sides of the river." This school would today be located about one and one-half miles southeast of Highland Institute at Guerrant, and approximately one-third of a mile from the mouth of Cow Branch. Another court order, dated June 2, 1879, appointed three men to review and mark the ground along which a road was proposed to begin "at the mouth of Bear Branch on Buckhorn and up the Bears Branch and by George Miller's schoolhouse and from said schoolhouse to the head of Nathan Miller's Branch." This school was on Fugate's Fork of Troublesome Creek in the vicinity where the Millers first settled when they came into what is now Breathitt County.

On Buckhorn Creek the community sponsored a school but had no schoolhouse. Teacher and pupils alike spread themselves out under a large shade tree and used sawed wooden blocks for seats. When it rained they ran to a near-by rock cliff for shelter.

Beginning Branch School, near present-day Athol, established around 1839 when Breathitt was made into a county, has the distinction of being the oldest, most continuously operated school in the county. When it was first established, it was operated upon the old subscription system. The original building of hand-hewn logs has been carefully removed from its original site to the campus of the modern two-story red brick high school of Breathitt County, in Jackson.

The War Between the States

The War between the States played havoc with the steady growth of a decade. School districts in Breathitt increased from twenty-nine in 1851 to forty-five in 1860, and the whole number of school-age children reported increased from 664 to 1,542 during the same period. Attendance fluctuated widely, for in 1860 the lowest number of pupils at school was 102, the highest number 755, and the average number 394. The greatest increase in the school census took place in 1852, the first year after the operation of the common schools, when 1,058 children of school age were reported.

In 1862, when military operations and wartime conditions had disrupted the normal flow of life, *only one school district reported.* In 1866 the newly appointed county school commissioner, W. M. Combs, reported that he "found districts and papers in bad condition," and that he "had not enough blanks for all the schools." In 1869 forty-two districts reported 2,290 school-age children; 1,145 as the highest number, 201 the lowest, and 640 as the average number at school.

Shortly after the close of the War between the States the first public colored school organized in Breathitt County was included under county statistics in the 1867 report of the state superintendent of public instruction. At that time forty pupils were enrolled in this school. The total Negro population of Breathitt in 1870 was only 181. Today (1940) there is only one Negro school in Breathitt County and it has an enrollment of fifty-five Negro pupils. The Negro population was 203 in 1930. Tuition was paid to the Jackson School Board for seven of these pupils who lived in the county.

"School-Keepin' and School-Goin' "

In the very early days it was customary at all the schools taught during J. Green Trimble's time:

for the scholars, when they desired a holiday, to do what they called "turning out the master." This consisted of the larger boys assembling at the schoolhouse early in the morning, fastening the door on the inside and refusing admittance to the teacher until a treaty could be negotiated. This always resulted in the capitulation of the teacher and the giving of a holiday. When this occurred at our school, three of the young men were appointed commissioners to agree upon terms, which resulted in the teacher agreeing to give a holiday of one day, furnish a bushel of mellow apples, ten pounds of candy, a gallon of whisky and sugar to sweeten it. [*Ibid.* p. 15.]

Another early incident revolving around the ethics of the code duello illustrates a more contemporary classroom problem—writing challenging, irritating remarks on the blackboard. At the time S. P. Ashford, of Woodford County, taught at the Beginning Branch School, blackboards were made from finished lumber that was painted black, and small blocks of wood with sheepskin tacked on were used to brush the chalk off the blackboard. On one occasion Mr. Ashford stepped out of the schoolhouse. During the teacher's absence some boy wrote a challenge on the blackboard reading, "to shoot at ten paces." Mr. Ashford became so enraged over this piece of anonymous effrontery that he exclaimed: "I'll give $10.00 to know of the *pahty* who wrote that challenge on the blackboard." Nothing ever came of the incident, however, as he never found out the identity of his challenger.

The teacher at the Combs school at Clayhole is said to have solved his disciplinary problems in an original fashion. Across the rafters of the building were laid poles. When the pupils misbehaved he would "hoist them up astride the poles" leaving them there until they agreed to better conduct. The early schoolmasters considered a dunce stool one of the most important pieces of school furniture. It was ordinarily a wooden block, high enough to allow the culprit who had been mischievous enough to get there to be seen by all his fellow pupils.

The schoolmaster conducted the school according to his own particular ideas about "school-keepin'." He selected his own supplies and planned the course of study. The teacher who could manage or lick the biggest boy in school, keep his pupils in their seats and at their books the entire school day, tolerate their crude pranks, and use the hickory stick freely was generally considered a good schoolmaster and was re-elected each year.

Slates were used up to the turn of the century. If there was a creek near by, the pupils would go down to give them an extra good scrubbing. Z. F. Smith, in his *History of Kentucky* (p. 174), mentions paddles or boards on which the ABC's were marked and which served a double purpose. These also have been mentioned in the reminiscences of old school teachers of Breathitt.

Under the pioneer conditions that prevailed all over Breathitt County, and that still prevail in numerous sections, teaching as well as attending school has been irregular. Cold weather, heavy rains, strong winds, and sudden unforeseen emergencies at home partly regulated the length of a school term as far as pupils were concerned. It takes enthusiasm, a pair of sturdy legs, and a strong constitution to walk anywhere from one to five miles to school in ankle-deep mud, in rain or snow, in cold weather, across rock ridges, down steep hillsides and flooded creeks, yet countless Breathitt pupils have done exactly this and continue to do it. This irregularity of attendance, however, has been one of the greatest drawbacks to the fuller and sounder education of Kentucky Mountain pupils. Sixty days for a long time was the standard attendance.

The schools in the mountains nearly all began after the crops had been "laid by." The attendance until about the middle of September was usually larger than at any other season. When the foddering season came, large numbers of pupils dropped out of school to gather their harvest, and their seats remained vacant the rest of the term. Other work was easily found when this was done or, as the sorghum season was so near, it was agreed that there was little to be learned by going back for so short a time and, when that work was over, the corn had to be gathered, and then school was so nearly out that all idea of going back was given up. The custom sprang up when there were no schools and the children, and in thousands of cases the women, too, were relied upon for this work.

In a letter to *The Jackson Times* (Nov. 18, 1924), the writer who lived in Jackson in 1892-95 remembered that "The attendance was very irregular. It was not uncommon for the attendance, after gathering fodder, to fall off to a very small number, and I have known instances where the teachers would go to the schoolhouse every morning for weeks and sometimes months when not a single one would meet him there, and he would go home and go to work."

Pupils studied Dilworth's or the "Blue-back" Speller, and when geography and arithmetic were taught it was more than likely without the use of text. Sometimes there were about as many classes as pupils, and between "calling up classes" the teacher would often read and tell stories. Spelling bees between the boys and girls were frequently held, and tended to further socialize the already well-socialized routine of the one-room schoolhouse. In the 1890's the McGuffey Readers were first introduced into Breathitt County. Geography, physiology, and grammar were added as a regular part of the curriculum of the county schools about this time. Blackboards and chalk were already then in general use; however, pupils still used slates and slate pencils.

Schoolbooks were brought in regularly with all other kinds of products and were sold by the local general merchant. Parents bought these books for their children. Practically the only reading available for pupils outside of their schoolbooks, and for older folks as well, was the weekly paper, an occasional magazine, and the Bible. There were no libraries, and books outside of texts were somewhat rare.

"Uncle Steve" Carpenter, of Noctor, before his death in December, 1939, related some of his early school teaching experiences in the little log building on Spring Fork. There was one bucket filled with water from the creek. A gourd was used as a dipper. "Uncle Steve" always sent his children to the creek at recess to wash their faces and hands. The most commonly played games included "marbles," "bull pen," a game similar to dodge ball, in which a wad of cotton was usually used for a ball, "go-sheepy go," and town ball. Marbles were never played for "keeps" but only for fun, and the side that cleared the most marbles from the ring won. Girls seldom took any active part in games at this time except in games of "tag."

A Half Century of Growth

The development of the school system after the War between the States continued to keep a fairly proportionate pace with the increasing population of the county and with the greater emphasis placed upon education and its wider diffusion among the people. The total number of pupils enrolled in county schools in 1899-1900, when the county population was 14,332, was 4,031. There were at that time eighty-two school districts. In 1911 the number of pupils had increased to 5,730. (Population, 17,540 in 1910 census.) At that time eighty-six schools had six-month terms and only three had school sessions less than six months. Five of the schools then had two or more teachers.

When the first statement on school buildings was published in the report of the superintendent of public instruction, in 1880, there were fifty-five log buildings and seventeen frame buildings in Breathitt County. In 1893 there were forty-one log schoolhouses, twenty-six frame schoolhouses, and one brick schoolhouse. Seven years later (1900-1901) there were sixteen log buildings and sixty frame buildings. No brick buildings were reported. During these two years eleven new schoolhouses were built and forty-nine repaired. The number of schoolhouses decreased during 1900-10, for in the 1911 biennial report of the school superintendent's report only three log and sixty-six frame schoolhouses were given.

Teachers of common schools were formerly paid according to the number of pupils in the school, and the length of the term sometimes depended on the number and attendance of the pupils. The pay varied from district to district. In 1894 Mr. Charles Terry taught on Puncheon Camp Creek for around $21 a month. The following year he taught at Oakdale where his monthly salary jumped to $63. Often, too, when there was no schoolhouse, a building was rented, and the rent usually had to be paid by the teacher.

The subscription schools which first fulfilled the meager educational needs of Breathitt flourished here and there in the county long after the common or county schools were started. Several of them continued up to 1920. They supplemented the short-term (three to five months) county schools and usually operated during the first several months of the year (January through March), while the common school term took in part of the summer and the fall. Some teacher would get up a "subscription" at the end of the regular school term and conduct a two- or three-month session. The fee for each pupil still ranged from $1.00 to $2.00 per month, usually the latter figure. When there were more than one pupil in a family, some kind of rate was usually given the parents. Some of these tuition fees were never paid, while that of some were paid in coal, wood, and by board. A few of these subscription schools during the latter part of the nineteenth century had as many as forty pupils. A subscription school started in February, 1940, at Elkatawa had an enrollment of forty pupils.

Lees College and the Church Schools

Lees College, organized as Jackson Academy in 1884 by Rev. J. J. Dickey, has been one of the most beneficial influences on education in the county. Under his direction it brought to bud a real interest in learning, and laid a solid foundation for the enlarged educational needs of Jackson and Breathitt County. When it was later taken over, first by Central University and then by the Kentucky Synod of the Presbyterian Church, it brought to a large area of the Kentucky Mountains the first curriculum embracing college subjects. From the beginning it has contributed innumerable teachers to Breathitt and adjoining counties. In this respect it was the pioneer in the upper Kentucky River basin.

Lees College has continued to play an important role in the educational life of Breathitt and the upper Kentucky River basin, particularly in the training of teachers. After the beginning of the twentieth century several church or so-called "missionary" schools were founded. The influence of these schools in their communities and on the character and outlook of their pupils has been one of the most civilizing factors in Breathitt County during the last few decades. Riverside Institute, at Lost Creek, was founded in 1906 by Mr. and Mrs. G. E. Drushal, Brethren missionaries. In 1908 Highland Institute at Guerrant was founded by Dr. E. O. Guerrant, a Presbyterian missionary. Mount Carmel Church School was established in 1925 by Rev. Lela G. McConnell. The Kentucky Mountain Bible Institute, associated with Mount Carmel, is the only school in Breathitt County today that offers courses in Greek. The Oakdale Vocational School, at Oakdale, was started as a grade school in 1920 by Miss Elizabeth E. O'Connor, a Free Methodist missionary, and in 1930 a high school department was added.

Today (1940) there are between eight and nine hundred pupils enrolled in the private schools of Breathitt County. Of these 269 were high school students. These schools, with their emphasis on Protestant Christian culture, have contributed much to the sturdiness and independence of the youth which they serve.

Schools in Jackson

The Jackson City School Board was not organized until August, 1910. Shortly after this, work was started on the present and only grade school building of Jackson which was completed in 1912. Before this, schools in Jackson had been a part of the county school system, but after this date they were under separate control.

Reminiscences of old schools and school teaching give an inkling of the changes that have taken place in Jackson. In the late seventies a school was taught in an old building located in "the Cutoff" and another one, a small log structure owned by Mrs. Evaline Hargis, wife of the late J. S. Hargis, was taught in a building on Main Street, on the opposite side of the street and about half a block above the courthouse. About 1880 a school was taught in an old building near the northern city limits along State 15 and on the site where a Primitive Baptist Church was located until 1934. The school was transferred from here to a building on Highland Avenue, a short distance southwest of the intersection of Highland Avenue and Jefferson Street and not far from Lees College. The school was conducted here until about 1895, when it was condemned and torn down in order to raise the level of the street after the top of this hill was leveled off. Mr. Farish Bach attended school in this old building from about 1891 to 1895, and later attended Lees College. When Mrs. Dora Blanton, assistant postmaster (1915-32), taught school in this same building her salary was $50 a month for a six-months term. The school was next moved to an old skating rink on Sycamore Street, near the corner of Main Street.

Mrs. Cora Noble, Breathitt County court clerk, taught school one year, probably 1907, in the old skating rink schoolhouse. She also taught school in the McCormack Chapel in South Jackson around 1908-9. This old building, which still belongs to Lees College, was rented to the city as a schoolhouse for the children of South Jackson. The school term was six months at this time. Lees College used to conduct a Sunday School and hold meetings in this building. Mr. Elijah Noble, her husband, taught school about 1908 with two other teachers in a building along about where Jerry Noble's building now stands. Rental on the building came out of the teachers' salary, which was about $31 per month.

Mrs. Noble attended the Highland Avenue School when her father, James L. Moore (d.1908), taught there. Mr. Moore belonged to the old school of self-educated schoolmasters—he never went to school a day in his life. When new subjects were introduced he studied up on them. For the greater part of forty years he taught the eight lower grades in both common and subscription schools in Jackson and in the county. Mr. Moore was an all-around character. At one time he was a magistrate. He was considered something of a doctor because he read medical books rather diligently, and a great many people came to him to be advised.

Changes and Progress During "The Thrilling Thirties"

When Mrs. Marie (Roberts) Turner was appointed county superintendent of schools, in 1932, she was the second woman to hold this office, Miss Cappie Little holding it during 1894-98. Mrs. Turner, a graduate of the high school department of Riverside Institute, at Lost Creek, her early home, taught school two years in Breathitt public schools and one year at Eclectic, Alabama. Then, in 1919, she married Mr. Ervine Turner, Jr., of Jackson, now state senator (1934-42) from the thirty-fourth senatorial district embracing Breathitt, Lee, Magoffin, Wolfe, and Morgan counties. ,

In 1932 there were 109 frame school buildings. Since then a program of consolidation, made possible through the Federal Work Relief program, has been pursued. Breathitt County now (1940) has 102 districts and 102 school buildings. Seventy-one of these are frame buildings; eleven, newly constructed one-room stone buildings; thirteen, two-room frame buildings; two, newly constructed two-room stone buildings; three, newly constructed three-room stone buildings; one, at Morris Fork, a two-story cement and frame school building with four classrooms, a large recreation hall, and a home economics room; and one, a six-room brick, at Caney. All these buildings are lighted with oil lamps and all but a few are heated with stoves.

There are now four consolidated schools in the county. Caney, a consolidation of Clayhole, Hard-shell, Caney, Buckhorn, and a part of Fugate's Fork was opened in 1934-35 in a six-room brick building. Lost Creek and Haddix, consolidated as Lost Creek in 1936, is housed in rented rooms of the old Riverside Institute building at Lost Creek, on State 15, where the early Lost Creek school has been housed since 1916. Big Rock, formed through the consolidation of Big Rock and Haddix Fork, was opened in 1937 in one of the new three-room stone structures. Vancleve, formed through the consolidation of Vancleve and Wilhurst, was opened in a new two-room stone building in 1938.

One of the most stimulating influences on education in Breathitt has been the program of guidance introduced several years ago. Outside contacts, round-table discussions, seminars, and publicity have created new interests and ideas. Mrs. Turner had long cherished an ambition of some day realizing educational standards for her native Breathitt comparable to other counties. She was anxious that the youth of Breathitt should understand and become qualified to cope with many of the problems peculiar to their county. Only one arterial highway had been constructed through Breathitt in 1932, and there is still only one hard-surfaced road through the county. Serious floods were almost an annual and sometimes a semiannual occurrence. The forests had been denuded of their timber to such an extent that the soil had lost its richness through erosion and was washed off the hillsides into the streams.

Dr. O. Latham Hatcher, founder and president of the Southern Women's Educational Alliance, later named the Alliance for Guidance for Rural Youth, with headquarters in Richmond, Virginia, had worked out her own guidance program and the studies of most value were introduced into schools aided by the alliance. In the fall of 1933, Mrs. Turner met Dr. Hatcher at the Southern Mountain Workers' Regional Conference held at the Robinson Substation, Quicksand. These two women soon discovered that they were interested in the same purposes. Dr. Hatcher arranged for a visit to some of the Breathitt County schools. A vocational specialist from Columbia University, together with Dr. Hatcher, conducted an occupational and educational survey of the county. Various agencies, including the T.V.A., the University of Kentucky, and the State Board of Education co-operated in this survey. As a result a guidance program was introduced into the Breathitt County schools, and in 1935 the State Board of Education gave official approval of the curriculum planned for Breathitt High School.

In 1935 music, home economics, agriculture, and in

1937 shop work were added to the curriculum, the last three being provided for through the Smith-Hughes bill. An art teacher, Mr. David Donoho, a graduate of the University of Kentucky, who had also studied in Paris and London, was added to the Breathitt High School faculty at this time. Other subjects include the "staples" of modern secondary education — English, mathematics, science, social science, and athletics.

Various student experiences of Breathitt High School pupils illustrate the values that modern schooling has been able to bring out in their lives and the promise of worthwhile living it holds out for the mountain boys and girls of Breathitt. Education can and does mean more to these students, for their world is more limited and their lives less varied than those of students in cities, modern towns, and in up-to-date agricultural communities. Association with the comparatively large student body and the faculty has in itself greatly benefited them. A new world with a greater number of possibilities has been opened to many of these students.

The most striking and certainly the most unexpected feature of the educational work done under this new program is in art. An art department offers work in a variety of media: drawing, water color painting, chalk drawing, linoleum block printing, mural painting, clay modeling, pottery making, and mask making. Drawing is done from memory, and from life—different students taking time about posing. In painting, students select the subject in which they are particularly interested, which is usually drawn from their daily experiences. In clay modeling, students make small statuettes or figurines suggested by interesting local characters. Useful objects such as vases, trays, and bookends are made from native clay. These are sometimes left undecorated and sometimes enriched with surface decorations of incised lines and modeled relief work. Subjects are adapted from the region—a mountain farmer, miner, peddler, or a simplified scene.

In all of the work which the art department undertakes there is always a conscious effort made to develop an original art expression native to the region, and with as much development as possible of individual abilities rather than the copying of either "pretty pictures" or real works of art. Students are discouraged from copying slick-surface details of nature or of other pictures with the idea of exhibiting work to dazzle school patrons with smooth-surface technique. Aside from their growth in art, the chief concern is that through expression in art these boys and girls will learn to analyze and interpret life according to their own background and understanding. Then, too, the byproducts of their art experiences and activities, such as the development of traits that are desirable in personality and character, are not to be overlooked.

The art department has been popular with a large part of the student body. Many are keenly interested and some show talent and originality. One of the art students, who found a very light gray, smooth textured clay on his home property, molds gracefully shaped vases in various designs from this clay and sells many of them. His father objected when he spent much of his time modeling, but when he sold some vases and other articles of pottery his father no longer objected.

Several crayon drawings by the best of Mr. Donoho's art students were exhibited at the Mayflower Hotel, Washington, D. C., during April 1937. Again, in 1938, an exhibit of work from the Breathitt High School studio was held at the National Art Gallery in Washington, D. C., including pottery and figurines and rural scenes. Mrs. Henry W. Morgenthau, wife of the U. S. Secretary of the Treasury, later displayed this work in her Capital City home.

The Agricultural Department of Breathitt High has sponsored a club of the Future Farmers of America, organized in 1935-36 with eighteen members and with a present (1940) membership of fifty-one. The poultry-judging team of this F.F.A. club won thirteenth place in the national contest at the American Royal Fair, Kansas City, Missouri, in 1938. This was quite an achievement when the poor quality of the county flocks is considered. At the annual State Fair in Louisville during the same year they took first place in the poultry contest. The club also enters the Harvest Festival held at the Robinson Substation, Quicksand, every year.

The F.F.A. makes an annual trip through the State. In 1938 thirty-one boys made a tour of the Bluegrass region, visited the Lexington airport, the stockyards, and horse farms. In 1939 the F.F.A. went to the State Fair

JACKSON AROUND 1890

at Louisville and to the State F.F.A. Convention in the same city. Each summer some members go to the F.F.A. camp at Harrodsburg. Their annual camping trip lasts one week to ten days. The club has a softball team and puts on a dance in the autumn and a banquet in the springtime.

The various departments in the Breathitt High School, especially home economics, natural science, and agriculture, are in a favorable position to make important contributions towards better homes and farms and to inculcate much needed ideas on sanitation and hygiene.

An Outlook: *Education to Tap Human Resources*

The ease with which education is now obtained in more highly developed districts obscures the difficulties which the early mountain pupils usually met in this connection. When, with many interruptions, they had learned to read and write, they had achieved a degree of education not common even then.

The story of education in Breathitt County today still carries a motif of individual sacrifices. Every school day, in dozens of simple homes tucked out of sight in hollows and overlooking creeks from hillside perches, lamplights flicker in the darkness of the early morning. City-folk are comfortably slumbering, and their milkman is making his rounds. But from these homes, where the fire is rekindled to prepare breakfast and where morning chores have to be performed before leaving for school, come the overalled boy and the girl dressed in cotton to learn more than their parents did. Some of them brave the inclemency of the worst winter weather to come to school. On many winter days, when it is dangerous for school busses to travel because of snow and ice, some of the high school students have walked part of the way and hitch-hiked the rest of the way to school.

After walking several miles down some creek road, they may ride anywhere from a few miles to ten miles on a school or a Greyhound bus. Many of them walk around five miles in the early part of the morning with a lantern in order to see the way. During the present school year (1939-40) a half dozen pupils from upper Hunting Creek, in the northeastern part of the county, travel eighteen miles to high school in Jackson.

Unlike city schools, where enrollments are expected to become more or less stationery and even to decline, and where school facilities for attendance have reached their highest development, there is still plenty of room for improvement in Breathitt County. Out of about 1,700 children of high school age approximately 700 attend high school. This difference is largely due to bad roads and lack of transportation facilities.

The schools and teachers of Breathitt are in a position to contribute greatly towards a general physical improvement and a wider range of knowledge and experience for the generation "coming up." In Breathitt, as in almost all mountain counties, the avenues of self-education and supplementary education, such as newspapers, magazines, the radio, and homes where there is a well-engraved heritage of education, play a minimum part in the education of most children. For this reason, the school can make larger, more valuable contributions. The natural resources of Breathitt have been almost totally exhausted but the county still has untapped and ever renewed human resources. It is probably from these alone that the more lasting wealth and values of Breathitt can be drawn tomorrow.

"MEETIN'-HOUSE" TO CHURCH

The religious background of the mountain pioneers was sectarian Protestantism—a highly individualistic religion, democratized and thinned by the continually advancing frontier. The Scotch, Irish, and English frontiersmen who swarmed over the New Land were altogether non-conformist. A few of them were Presbyterians, some were Methodists but the larger body were "Hard-shell" Baptists. Undoubtedly many of them who trod winding mountain trails and wilderness paths to take up their abode in the Kentucky foothills carried among their scant belongings a Bible. Since there were no churches at first, meetings were held in the homes and, when the weather permitted, out in the open. The earliest church was the rude fireplace of the pioneer's cabin; the earliest congregation, his family; the first services, readings from the Bible.

When Breathitt County was formed, the only organized church was that of the Hard-shell Baptists. Their church building was located on the north side of Quicksand about six hundred yards above its mouth, and near the ford. The branch emptying into Quicksand Creek near the church building was appropriately named "Meetin'-house Branch."

The Hard-shell or Regular Baptists formed the principal denomination in the mountains during the period of early settlements and in some sections even today. Historically the Hard-shell Baptist Church was perhaps more adapted to the religious needs of the mountaineer of an earlier day than the more formalized denominations. It originated on the North Carolina frontier shortly after the middle of the eighteenth century. It soon began to organize itself into associations in most of the Southern States because of the difficulties of travel in the mountains and the scarcity of church buildings. Theologically, it is Calvinistic, practically all believing in predestination and some in infant damnation. The Hard-shell Baptists do not believe in Sunday schools, missionary movements, or salaried ministers. The minister of the gospel must be "called" and go forth to preach without any preparation whatever. He need not be able to read or write. For these reasons, it is sometimes also known as the Primitive Baptist Church.

A humorous story often told on himself by Mason Williams, who married into the Breathitt Copes, illustrates the humane attitude which mountain people still take towards denominationalism. Mr. Williams, a native of Morgan County, was a preacher and politician. On one of his campaign trips many years ago, in the Big Sandy Valley, he was invited to stay over with one of his brethren to preach on Sunday. When he arrived at the home of his host, who was unable to accompany him, he found two or three neighboring women there. After awhile he laid down under a shade tree to rest and cool off, since it was a hot July day, and he shortly fell asleep.

As he lay there an argument started among the women in the house as to what denomination he represented. It was conceded that he was not sufficiently well dressed to be a Presbyterian minister, also that his horse was too poor for a Methodist circuit-rider. Another suggested that he might be a Mormon disciple, some of whom were then traveling over the country. Finally one of them remarked that she could soon settle the question by examining his hymn books, and she ran her hands into his saddle-bags which were lying in the room, to find his hymn-book. The first thing her hand encountered was a quart bottle of whiskey. She held it up and exclaimed: "Oh, he's an old hard-shelled Baptist; here is his bottle of whiskey," which was taken as conclusive evidence.

J. Green Trimble received this story directly from Mr. Williams (*Recollections,* pp. 6-7).

The Methodist Church was one of the first to do missionary work in this county. Since the number of preachers was small and the territory to be covered large, each minister was given a sizable area known as a circuit. He usually had four points where he preached and evangelized. The circuit rider visited each point once a month. A presiding elder traveled from one circuit to another helping the local preacher, and holding a protracted meeting once a year at each of the points. Both the presiding

"MEETIN'-HOUSE" TO CHURCH

elder and the circuit rider rode horseback from place to place and boarded among the friends of the church.

Around 1835 Rev. R. W. Landrum, a young preacher of twenty-one, accepted the "Wilderness Circuit" as his first assignment from the Methodist Conference in session in Clark County. Although young and inexperienced, he accepted the task of covering a circuit that embraced Whitesburg, Hazard, the Forks of Troublesome (Hindman), and part of what is now Breathitt County. He married during his first year's work and some years later settled at the mouth of Lost Creek, the center of Breathitt's salt industry. After settling in Breathitt, Rev. R. W. Landrum, assisted by Elkanah Johnson and Samuel P. Chandler, organized a number of Methodist churches in the county. Rev. Mr. Landrum, however, preached mostly in the church built at Lost Creek, around 1850, by Lewis Campbell, and known as "Liberty" Church because anyone, regardless of denomination, could preach there.

In 1851 Rev. Nathan Arrowood came across the mountains from Buncombe County, North Carolina. After a brief stay on Red Bud, now in Clay County, he settled with his family on Wolf Branch of Canoe Creek. Shortly after he settled here, Rev. Mr. Arrowood established the "Regular" Baptist Church in the upper Middle Fork region with the assistance of Jacob Midcalf. They secured assistance from the Buncombe County Baptist Church and established the Regular Baptist Church at Canoe, which is still in existence. This is considered the first Regular Baptist Church in this section of the Middle Fork. Many others were established around this time and afterwards in Breathitt and neighboring counties. These churches today make up the Mountain Association.

The Christian Church, first introduced into Bourbon County in 1832, and known originally as the Campbellite Church, was the third denomination to make a religious imprint on Breathitt. The first minister of that church to deliver a sermon in Breathitt County was Rev. Joseph Nickell. He was a successful evangelist noted for having baptized more converts and married more couples than any preacher of his age in Kentucky. When Breathitt County was formed, the nearest Christian Church was at Hazel Green where one of the most distinguished and earliest ministers of this church, "Raccoon" John Smith, preached. Among "Raccoon" Smith's hearers at one of his preachings was a young school teacher, Nixon Covey, who came from Montgomery County to Hazel Green in 1839 to teach school. J. Green Trimble (*Ibid., p.* 11) reports that he was considered a wicked and dissipated man. He was converted and joined the church at this meeting, and then he"commenced preaching the next day, and continued to preach until his death . . . He taught school in Breathitt County until about the beginning of the Civil War."

An early member of the Christian Church in Breathitt was the rather remarkable and very religious "Aunt Milly" Cockrell, widow of John Cockrell, one of the pioneering Cockrell brothers. Aunt Milly attended three or four annual meetings held at Hazel Green by Rev. Mr. Smith, a great favorite of hers. In the summer months for several years during the 1830's, she rode horseback through a sparsely inhabited wilderness to attend church at Hazel Green, a distance of twenty-one miles from her home.

When John Hunt Morgan passed through Breathitt County on a campaign trip to the Bluegrass on the sixth and seventh of June, 1864, there was a young soldier in his ranks who stored up disturbing impressions of the Southern Highlands. This man, E. O. Guerrant, later returned as a physician, and still later as a minister of the gospel.

According to his own account, Dr. Guerrant was brought up in a village of churches and as a result he thought everybody this side of China was equally blest. His interest in the Highlands began when he rode more than a hundred miles across the mountains to Virginia to join the Army. As quoted by Ernest Trice Thompson in *Presbyterian Missions in the Southern United States* (p. 225), Dr. Guerrant reported: "Although not looking for churches or preachers, I do not remember seeing a single one. During the year I crossed those mountains several times and still found no churches. After the War I became a physician and frequently rode through those mountains, visiting the sick, and still found only a church or two in many miles . . . "

Dr. Guerrant shortly thereafter gave up the practice of medicine to enter Union Theological Seminary. During a sick spell, it is said, Dr. Guerrant vowed that he would devote his life to preaching the gospel to the poor if he became well. As pastor of churches near the Highlands and then of the First Presbyterian Church of Louisville, he repeatedly pointed out to the synod the destitution of the mountains, and reminded it of the culpable neglect of the church in not sending them the gospel.

When the Synod of Kentucky embarked upon its plan of home missions, in 1881, Dr. Guerrant resigned his comfortable pastorate in Louisville to become one of the first missionaries. He was assigned the eastern part of the State, including the mountain country. Dr. Guerrant later said that he thought he had some idea of the vast destitution of the mountain regions, "but when I entered the work I was amazed to find a region as large as the German Empire practically without churches, Sabbath schools or qualified teachers; whole counties with tens of thousands of people who had never seen a church or heard a Gospel sermon they could understand."—[*Loc. cit.*]

Dr. Guerrant is said to have been a veritable tongue of flame passing through the narrow valleys and along the tortuous waterways of eastern Kentucky. His first sermon in Breathitt was preached in the log school building at Beginning Branch, near Athol, around 1881. He next went to Frozen Creek where he established a church near the place of William Day, Sr. Later he returned to the Middle Fork section of the county and established a church on the Spicer Farm near Jetts Creek. From there he went out to various points: Elkatawa, Canoe, Shoulderblade, Rousseau, and Jackson. He left a worker at each place and afterwards only supervised these points.

Dr. Guerrant headed the Home Mission Society for twenty-five years and otherwise served a large section of the mountain people of Kentucky. Early in his apostolic career he realized that no lasting results could be achieved in religious culture unless there was an educational basis to sustain it and trained leaders to continually nourish it. Primary schools were started sometimes in a log building and at other times in a tent or under a tree. For the most part these schools were small and held only in the summer. Highland Institute was one of the seven boarding schools he helped establish in Kentucky. Another outstanding one was Stuart Robinson at Blackey, in Letcher County, Kentucky. In addition to churches, mission centers, and schools Dr. Guerrant also founded an orphanage in connection with Highland Institute.

Another one of "Morgan's Men" who became an outstanding missionary in Breathitt was "Uncle Ben" Biggerstaff. He was not a preacher in the regular sense and he never resided in the county. "Uncle Ben" made regular trips to the mountains from the Bluegrass. Each time he brought something that would improve conditions in this section—purebred chickens, hogs, and cattle. These were exchanged for things which the people could spare. While here he was always busy with his Sunday school and social work. Indicative of the zeal of "Uncle Ben" was his remark that he would rather be superintendent of a Sunday school than President of the United States.

Shortly after Dr. Guerrant began his missionary endeavors in the mountain section of eastern Kentucky, one of the most notable men in the history of the county, J. J. Dickey, of Flemingsburg, Kentucky, accidentally located in Jackson. He was a Methodist circuit rider who shortly after his arrival became a teacher, and several years later a journalist. Rev. Mr. Dickey founded Lees College and for a number of years edited *The Jackson Hustler* in the most vigorous manner. He was one of the ablest preachers who ever mounted a rostrum in Breathitt County. The variety of his activities, his forceful, outspoken opinions, for which he suffered, made him unsurpassed as a civic leader. He organized Sunday schools, preached in Jackson and at other points in the county.

After Dr. Guerrant and Rev. Mr. Dickey, other missionaries selected some spot in the Breathitt hills to carry on their religious work. Soon after the turn of the century Rev. and Mrs. G. E. Drushal, missionaries of the United Brethren in Christ, a Protestant sect founded in the United States in 1800, came to Lost Creek. Here they established Riverside Institute and a Brethren Church and Sunday school. Since then, Brethren churches and Sunday schools have been organized at various points in the county.

Another church school around which missionary activities center is the Oakdale Vocational School which originated in the religious work started in 1919 by Miss Elizabeth O'Connor, a missionary of the Free Methodist Church. Since then all the work of this church has been conducted from Oakdale. In addition to the church at this point, there are seven mission centers, five of them with church buildings, and seven Sunday schools conducted by Oakdale. The Free Methodist Church, a fundamentalist sect, was founded at Pekin, New York, in 1860, and had its origin in certain differences with the Genesee Conference of the Methodist Church. It claims to have preserved the original doctrines of Methodism undiluted with modern trends.

In the summer of 1924 another outstanding woman missionary, Lela G. McConnell, an ordained elder of the Methodist Church, came to Breathitt County. With two students from Asbury College, Wilmore, Kentucky, she first conducted revival meetings in schoolhouses, carrying with her a folding organ. Mount Carmel School was founded during the year. The work started by Miss McConnell grew, year by year. Mount Carmel is now the center for twenty-two preaching points located in the extreme rural sections of six different counties of the mountains of eastern Kentucky. There are church buildings and parsonages in twelve of the twenty-two preaching points, and a continuous building program extends Mount Carmel's church work into many neglected parts of Breathitt and other counties.

The religious pattern of Breathitt today is somewhat different from that of most non-mountainous sections of the country. Outside of Jackson, it is still largely a missionary county. There is a weakness, too, for sectarianism seems to be congenial with the individualism of the mountaineer. A number of small sects, practically unknown in other sections of the country, play an important part in the religious life of the county. Only two or three nationally known churches, the Presbyterian being the most outstanding, noticeably figure in the religious life of Breathitt. It is interesting that today in the whole of Breathitt County there is not a single Catholic or Jew. The religion of the mountaineer is also inclined to be superstitions and to have a mystical, melancholy strain. In the past it usually had a slight touch of antinomianism, which is still evident today. Sporadic religious emotionalism of the revival type is another characteristic of mountain religion.

In retrospect Breathitt has been handicapped in the

development and maintenance of churches in the same way that it was held back in schools during the early days. There is little money to support regular pastors, or for suitable church buildings. The rugged nature of the country limits the size of the congregation and lowers church attendance during a part of the year. The resulting irregularity lessens interest. The organization of the Presbyterian Church, one of the most favorable examples, gives an idea of this situation. There are (1940) six churches and seven mission centers of this denomination in Breathitt but only about six hundred members. Nevertheless, Sunday schools, churches, and church schools exist today in every section of the county. Morris Fork is an outstanding example of church work in one of Breathitt's most isolated communities.

PART II. POINTS OF INTEREST

POINTS OF INTEREST IN JACKSON AND ENVIRONS

1. COUNTY COURTHOUSE, "the heart of Breathitt County," is a two-story red brick building of nondescript style, now decaying and dilapidated on the inside. It was erected in 1886-87, but since then several improvements, including an addition in 1912, have been made. The bell in the tower is rung in the morning and afternoon for the convening of circuit court, when it is in session, and on other special occasions. The tower clock has not been wound for years and on each of its four faces shows a different time. The building houses two courtrooms and all the court offices of the county, including those of the county attorney and judge, and the circuit and county court clerks. It was from the tower of this building that a gunman, Hen. Kilburn, and a young Negro were lynched at its entrance, and in 1903 that J. B. Marcum was slain. A two-room building that once stood beside an earlier courthouse was used as the office of the circuit and county court clerks and as a depository for county records. When it was burned, around 1873, to destroy certain forged deeds as was thought, only the first circuit court orderbook covering the period 1839-49 was saved. This book has much quaint information in it including bounties for wolf scalps. Among the curious items entered in county documents is the court order "that Grandvill Polly, a pauper of this County be let out at public out cry at the court house door in the town of Jackson on the third Monday in November 1879 — To the loudest bidder and that the sheriff will act as comr. [commissioner] in said cause and county judge make allowance for same."

2. A MARKER of stuccoed cement and pyramidal in form was erected in the northwest corner of the Courthouse Square by the Jackson Chapter of the Sons of the

American Revolution in 1936. All the charter members of this chapter, whose names are inscribed on a bronze tablet, trace their ancestry to Nathan Brittain, a private in Capt. Jonathan Clark's company of the Eighth Virginia Regiment, Col. Abraham Bowman commanding.

3. COUNTY JAIL in Courthouse Square facing College Avenue, is a two-story sandstone building in Colonial style completed in February, 1940. The building was begun in 1939 as a joint county and Federal Work Relief project and completed at a cost of approximately forty thousand dollars. Eight hundred and forty perches of stone at ten cents a perch were used in its construction. The stone, of rough face and laid in broken ashlar with double fan work, was quarried on Butler's Branch, about four miles from Jackson. The building has the most modern appointments of a "small-time" jail, includes an apartment for the county jailer, and cells for women and the county's Federal prisoners. The floors and roof in the jail section of the building are of reinforced concrete. Interior stone walls are twenty inches thick, while the outside walls from the basement up to the first floor are eighteen inches thick, and from the first floor to the roof sixteen inches thick. The windows have metal casings and fireproof glass. A wag in Jackson, mindful of the county's feud past, has remarked on the jail: "The very best for Breathitt's leading citizens."

4. THE BACH MEMORIAL HOSPITAL, a two-story building of stuccoed stone, erected in 1914, contains twelve rooms including an operating room and various types of hospital equipment such as an X-ray machine. It is now a memorial to its founder, Dr. Wilgus Bach, who was one of Breathitt County's most prominent civic minded citizens. Dr. Bach was one of the four sons of Hiram Bach of the Stevenson community of this county who became M.D.'s. It is now the only hospital in Breathitt County equipped for regular hospitalization.

5. LEES JUNIOR COLLEGE, at the intersection of Jefferson and College streets, is a coeducational institution that has distinguished itself in various respects since its founding over a half century ago. It was the pioneer in a more advanced, comprehensive secondary education in the mountains of southeastern Kentucky, and for many

years had the only brick schoolhouse in the region. Somewhat later it was the only institution of collegiate standing between Winchester and the Virginia line. From the beginning it has served a large region as a normal school.

Lees College has again assumed a unique and pioneering role in bringing to worth-while mountain boys and girls a two-year college education without regard to financial ability. Since 1937, under the direction of its president, J. O. VanMeter, Lees College has conducted a unique experiment in financing the education of the mountain youth of the upper Kentucky River Basin which it serves. At that time it inaugurated a policy of accepting notes from students of good character and at least average scholarship who were unable to pay their way through the first two years of college. During the first two years of this daring plan over $20,000 in IOU's were accepted and all but $1,800 has already been paid.

Lee's five-acre campus extends over the landscaped greensward of a leveled slope. Two brick buildings, set off in clumps of evergreen shrubbery, house the entire college plant. The older of the two, a two-story brick structure weathered into soft, gray tones, was erected in 1887. Administrative offices as well as classrooms are located here. The modern three-story building is used principally as a dormitory. It also houses the college's 4,000-volume library, recreation quarters, including a gymnasium, and the usual facilities of a boarding school such as dining-hall, kitchen, and laundry.

Lees College has a storybook beginning as interesting as its present-day plan of financing the education of its mountain students is daring. About the year 1880, Rev. John J. Dickey, a Methodist preacher, of Flemingsburg, Kentucky, on his way to Perry County, rode into Jackson astride a lame horse. When he stopped here he asked Mr. G. W. Sewell, the first man he encountered, where he could find a place to put up for the night and have his horse cared for. Mr. Sewell took him to his home and his horse to his stable. After taking care of the horse and attending to the travel-worn stranger's personal needs, they proceeded to get acquainted. Mr. Dickey told of his desire to establish a school in the mountains, and his newly-made friend told him he could not find a better place than Jackson. Mr. Dickey agreed, and the home of Mr. Sewell became his home, for he located at Jackson where he began teaching a private school in the courthouse.

While teaching in this makeshift school, he conceived the idea of establishing a mountain college at Jackson. In 1884 he was granted a charter by the Kentucky General Assembly to establish a school to be known as Jackson Academy, with powers allowing indefinite expansion of curriculum and influence. Through his untiring efforts and zeal, he finally succeeded at the end of three years in raising enough money in Jackson and Breathitt County to purchase the land and erect the first building. William E. Dodge, a New York philanthropist, contributed to the academy shortly after it was established and for several years provided tuition for a number of its students.

Mr. Dickey himself helped build the old Academy Building, which is still standing today. Brick for the building was made by hand and baked on the spot. The walls, floors, and roof had been completed in the winter of 1887. In Mr. Dickey's journal, part of which is now in the possession of Lees College, there is a glimpse of the man's unbounded courage and zeal. On Wednesday, December 21, he wrote: "Tonight after church I went back to the academy and kept up the fires, to keep the plaster from freezing, till ten o'clock." On December 24: "The past three nights I have been attending church and keeping up the fires in the academy to prevent the plastering from freezing and have not therefore had time to write in my journal."

The cost of the building and grounds was $6,280. After the completion of its new building, Mr. Dickey acted as principal of Jackson Academy for four more years. In 1891 it was sold to Central University of Richmond, Kentucky, under a judgment to satisfy a debt of $2,280, and its name altered to the Jackson Collegiate Institute. It was developed into a regular college and conducted with a marked degree of success for sixteen years by that university. Large sums of money were given by Mrs. Cyrus H. McCormick, of Chicago, Illinois, and Mrs. Susan P. Lees, of New York. In 1893 Mrs. Lees placed the school on a firm foundation for the remainder of her life by large donations, and the name shortly thereafter was changed to S. P. Lees Collegiate Institute. In October, 1906, the school passed from the control of Central University to

JACKSON TODAY

the Kentucky Synod of the Presbyterian Church (Southern Assembly), and since then has remained under its ownership and control.

The mountain boys and girls who attend Lees College are a fairly serious, up-to-date lot. Many of them come from scraggly, soil-depleted mountain farms where nothing but hardships have ever been known. Most of them finish with teaching diplomas which enable them to secure teaching positions in the mountain counties without much difficulty. Its student body of 264 in 1938-39 was drawn from eighteen mountain counties including Breathitt.

6. THE COMMUNITY PLAYGROUND, part of the five-acre campus of Lees College, was built as a municipally sponsored Federal Work Relief project. It was completed in 1939 at a cost of approximately $50,000. The two sections of its concrete stadium, known as "Barkley Bowl," seat 6,000 people. The retaining walls are of native limestone, the one on the south side being 150 feet long and 22 feet high. Until it was first filled in, around 1933, this part of the campus was a hollow.

7. JACKSON CITY HIGH SCHOOL (R) AND GRADE SCHOOL (L), two brick buildings of a similar construction, overlook the Community Playground and the campus and buildings of Lees College. The grade school, completed in 1912, is a two-story building of modern construction and appointments. It has a full basement, a cafeteria, nine classrooms, an auditorium with a seating capacity of 510, and a small stage. In 1938-39 it had an enrollment of 375 and a faculty of eight teachers. The Jackson City High School, also a two-story brick building with a full basement, was erected in 1928. It has a gymnasium with a regulation floor, a library containing 1,100 volumes, and five classrooms. The enrollment in 1938-39 was 148 with a faculty of five teachers. The Jackson City High School is accredited by the Association of Kentucky Colleges and Secondary Schools.

8. BREATHITT COUNTY HIGH SCHOOL, at the foot of Court Street, a two-story T-shaped building of stone-trimmed red brick, is one of the most up-to-date county high schools in the mountains of eastern Kentucky. It was erected through the aid of Federal Work Relief at a cost of $67,000, with equipment costing $12,000. Its

curriculum as well as its newly constructed plant, including a gymnasium and workshops and the modern transportation facilities provided for its pupils, place it in the front rank of Breathitt's recent development.

The ten-acre campus occupies part of the meadow once known as the "Hargis Bottoms." The school's three-acre lawn has been filled in to raise it about eight feet above the flood line, which is about twenty feet higher than the normal level of the river at this point. Young saplings of black gum, umbrella, red maple, sourwood, and yellow poplar, all native to Breathitt hills, have been planted on the grounds, while in front there is a row of old maples.

The new Breathitt High School was opened to students during the fall of 1937. A separate county high school, first located at Quicksand, was opened with an enrollment of thirty pupils in September, 1927. The enrollment for 1937-38 was 279, and for 1938-39, 310 students.

The building was dedicated by the wife of the President, Mrs. Franklin D. Roosevelt, on February 27, 1939, when the entire mountain region was in the grip of the most severe weather of that winter. When it appeared that the First Lady, who had journeyed to Lexington to attend the twenty-fourth annual Farm and Home Convention, would be unable to travel over the snow and ice-bound highway with her party of notables, the trip to Jackson was canceled. The county school superintendent, Mrs. Marie R. Turner, thereupon organized a committee which raised enough money to charter a special train to Jackson. In spite of the forbidding weather, a crowd of 2,000 jammed the school auditorium. Most of them were mountain folk who made hazardous journeys over ice-coated roads to welcome the First Lady. The dedication program, over which the high school principal, Mr. R. M. Van Horne, presided, was entirely in the hands of the pupils.

9. The PANHANDLE AND PANBOWL, one of the most fascinating spots in the environs of Jackson, is reached either by crossing the swinging or footbridge, at the foot of Court Street, or by crossing the highway bridge into South Jackson and then following the narrow dirt road that leads through the "Cutoff" and branches left

on to the Panhandle and Panbowl. When seen from Jackson, the Panhandle has the appearance of a sway-back ridge. At each end stone outcroppings tower starkly above the "saddle" of this narrow strip like relentless sentries on strategically placed forts. Long famous as a curious natural phenomenon, it is the stem of that fan-shaped section of land around which the North Fork flows and almost returns upon itself. The swing begins at the bend of the river in the lower part of the town. Here many decades ago the river is said to have kept a straight course through the narrow defile of the Cutoff until it was filled in. The North Fork, from this point to a point where it swings away from the Cutoff on the opposite side, makes a detour of about seven miles. At the Panhandle Tunnel the ridge is only about fifty or sixty feet wide from base to base, while the tunnel itself is around forty feet in length. From this vantage a panoramic view of Jackson and the surrounding country can be obtained. A variety of scenery unfolds in every direction. The North Fork flows gently on both sides. The fairly fertile bottom lands on the far side of the river, the swinging bridges that span it on both sides, the coal mine at the western end of the Cutoff, the wild vegetation and rugged outlines of the Panhandle, and the drab house on the bottom land below the tunnel, with its cow pen and pigsty, form a pattern in which natural beauty blends with human color.

The wagon road leading across the Panhandle forks when it reaches the rocks that stairstep to the top of the cone-shaped Panbowl Hill. The path that continues straight on up to the top branches at one point to the right and left. These branches lead to rock houses, one a deep but low sheltered rock ledge. "Indian Postoffice," the other rock house, is not as deeply sheltered as the first, but it has a naturally formed rock seat and numerous frost-eroded "pigeonholes." The name, "Indian Post-office," was given to it because these pigeonholes, which suggest post office boxes, are sometimes used by the boys and girls of Jackson to exchange "blind" notes. The word "Indian" seems to have been tacked on to give it a primitive flavor. At another point this path extends for about twenty-five feet over a narrow strip, or "razorback," just wide enough for a foothold. Along the path there is a large, flat-topped boulder which affords a sweeping vista of the surrounding country. The topmost part of the hill, less rugged than the lower part, is covered with trees and sod. Beyond this point a series of smaller hills slope toward the bottom lands that rim the North Fork around the bend.

The Panhandle and Panbowl touch off fanciful currents in the imagination. Myriad forms and colors, fantastically shaped rocks, half-veiled in the foliage of evergreens and the profusion of shrubs, form a wild symphony of nature. At sunset on windy days there is a Promethean touch to contemplation atop the largest of the cliffs. It is a heady spot where some ancient spirit still seems to brood. The Panhandle and Panbowl are equally suited to poetry, philosophy, romance, murder, or just plain exercise.

THE PANHANDLE TUNNEL, cut through the solid rock partition of the Panhandle, furnished water power for a mill which stood here until about 1906. The tunnel, around twenty-five feet wide by thirty feet high and thirty-five or forty feet in length, utilized a fall of seven feet in the stream bed.

The Panhandle Mill was established, according to local tradition, before the War between the States. A large gate was pulled up to let the water flow against the wooden wheel which turned its machinery. The mill was a three-story wooden building, built entirely with hand tools. Logs were caught on the first floor; on the second floor there were mills for lumber and grain, and machinery for weaving; the third floor was used for storage. Ten thousand feet of lumber a day could be sawed at this mill which was considered one of the most powerful in this region. Flax and even cotton were woven into cloth, and hemp was made into bagging. Looms and spinning wheels, operated by foot, were used for light weaving, and water power was used for heavy weaving. The seeds were removed from the different plants and usually the stuff was carded before it was brought to the mill. A Negro who worked at the mill during its last years received ten cents a day and his board for "cranking" a machine all day long. In 1898 the mill was partly destroyed by high water, and after this it was never repaired. By 1906 it had been completely wrecked by high water.

Even farmers from adjoining counties are said to

have brought their wheat and corn here to be ground. A two-day trip to the mill, a day or so in Jackson, and then two days back home made "going to the mill" a long, leisurely task for those who lived a distance. In the memories of old-timers in Jackson, the charge for grinding grain toward the latter part of the last century was one-eighth of each bushel.

An old-fashioned shooting-match sometimes diverted the men who were gathered in Jackson for business at the mill. A shooting-match was the favorite sport of the mountaineer. The prize was sometimes a fat beef but usually a hog. When the latter, the best shot received the hams; the second best, the shoulders; the third best, the sides, heart, liver, etc.; the fourth best, the hide and tallow. The man who won the two hams usually treated with one of them. Peach and apple brandy were plentiful, and added to the attractions of "going to the mill."

10. The CUTOFF is a defile or narrow valley extending from the bend of the river on the Jackson side to its meandering return on the other side of the hill. The railroad enters Jackson through the Cutoff. Except on the two ends where it is open to the river, it is shut in by steep hills. Dingy wooden houses, many of them now abandoned, dot the hillsides. Most of the people who live in this section depend for a living on the coal mine overlooking the North Fork at the far end of the Cutoff.

11. The FEDERAL BUILDING, on West Broadway, a three-story structure of cream-colored brick, was completed in 1916 at a cost of approximately $125,000. It was built while J. W. Langley was United States Senator from eastern Kentucky and replaced the post office burned in the Hallowe'en fire of 1913. The building houses such Federal agencies as the U. S. Post Office, an Army Recruiting Office, and court rooms; and also the offices of the County Health Board and the county agricultural agent. The stone used for the window trimming and decorative insets was carved and brought in from near-by Rowan County.

12. The STIDHAM HOME, on Broadway beyond the Federal Building, is a spacious two-story red brick residence built around 1885 by Charles J. Little, a Jackson merchant. The brick was hand-made and burned on the ground near the site of the house, and the woodwork was

hand-tooled. The colored glass in its hall doors was set in when the house was erected. This was the first brick house in Jackson and one of the first, if not the first, in Breathitt County. Jack Rawlings, a Confederate soldier, of Mount Sterling, Kentucky, designed and constructed the house. Fruit trees of different kinds, a half-acre vegetable garden, and a row of maple trees in front give the house a pleasing setting. Mr. Little, the original owner, sold the property in 1904 to his wife's brother, John E. Patrick. Mr. M. S. Crain purchased the house around 1918, and its present occupant, Mr. J. L. Stidham, a lawyer, purchased it in 1926.

13. SNAKE VALLEY, through which State 15 (here united with State 30) makes its southern exit from Jackson, was once the "skid row" of the county. Drinking, gambling, and bawdiness flourished along this stretch during the town's heyday. Until recently (1940) a roadside tavern was named "The Bloody Bucket," and is still known as such by the inhabitants.

POINTS OF INTEREST IN THE COUNTY

1. FROZEN MOUNTAIN (1,500 alt.), three miles north of Jackson, is one of the most panoramic spots along State 15. The highway winds in great loops up the steep hillside, permitting the motorist or the hiker to look down on two sections of the road which he had just passed or will soon pass. At the top precipitous cone-shaped mountains extend on all sides as far as the eye can see into the hazy distance. Hollows, the narrow V-shaped valley that drains into the North Fork of the Kentucky River, and then the bottom lands of the Panbowl, add to the pleasing contrast of the landscape. Here in every direction are scenes typical of Breathitt.

Profusely scattered among its wooded hillsides are all the varieties of wild flowers, of shrubs and trees that make the mountainous countryside an everchanging delight. In the early spring the hillsides, starred with the white blooms of the servicetree, are resplendent with yellow sassafras and the varying purplish tones of the redbud or, as some of the mountain people call it, "the Judas tree." Before the redbud has shed its brilliant dress for a more sober garb of small green leaves, the luxuriant ivory blooms of dogwood, resembling patches of snow, suddenly appear.

The maple, oak, poplar, and beech, together with an undergrowth of clambering wild grapevines, sumac, wild peas, and finely pinnated ferns transform the bleak, winter-swept hillsides into mammoth billows of variously hued green. The air is scented with the fragrance of the honeysuckle, the blossoms of the wild crabapple and plum trees, and an occasional honeylocust. The trailing-arbutus, with its white perfumed flowers, covers the brows of cliffs, and the laurel ("ivy" of the mountaineer) roots itself in the crevices of sheer rock, while the rhododendron ("laurel" of the mountaineer) flourishes in deep, moist hollows below.

The wild pansy of velvety blue, the yellow buttercup, the pink skullcap, and the dark red of the Indian or devil's-paintbrush mottle the emerald of the more secluded countryside. Blue, white, and yellow violets grow here and there in protected spots of rich soil. The wild sweet-william, with its lilac clusters, grows mostly around big trees and reaches about half the height of the cultivated plant, while the wild iris, or flag, also reaching little more than half the height of the cultivated plant, grows along streams in high yet moist places.

Blackberry, raspberry, and to a lesser extent wild gooseberry bushes grow, especially in uncleared woodlands. Other berry plants include the dewberry, the huckleberry, the buckberry, and the elderberry. All these berries are gathered and eaten except the elderberry which some mountain people think is poisonous while a few others use it in making wine.

As the autumn days approach, a plant with grayish, rough-textured leaves and a star-shaped cluster of dark blue flowers, appears and is named "farewell-to-summer." In the fall the hills of Breathitt are ablaze with a riot of color, as though splashed from the brush of a great painter who has lavished over the landscape the glory of his palette. Trees and shrubbery, turning into the brilliance of storybook pictures, become rich jewels of ruby, amber, dusty rose, topaz, and gold. Hanging from tree trunks like necklaced pendants of deep-toned amethyst are clusters of wild grapes. As the radiant foliage fades and falls, the evergreens, among them the red-berried holly-tree and the mistletoe, are best appreciated. The long, straight shafts of hemlocks or spruce pines usually found in rock-walled hollows give a touch of classic beauty to their locale. Other pines and cedar dot occasional hills, and in clumps and groves stand out in pleasant contrast to the gray, winterish landscape.

2. MOUNT CARMEL, located at Lawson, thirteen miles from Jackson, in the northwestern part of the county at the confluence of Mill Creek and the North Fork, is the home of the Mount Carmel Church School and the Kentucky Mountain Bible Institute.

THE KENTUCKY MOUNTAIN BIBLE INSTITUTE, established in 1931, was first located at Vancleave on State 15 in a large three-story building until the "flash" flood of July, 1939. At that time the quarters of the institute were swept away and one of the professors, his three children, two students, and three visitors were drowned. It was then moved to its present location on land donated by Mr. and Mrs. Fred Fletcher and Laura Fletcher Walters, along the Mount Carmel Road. Rebuilding on the present site began on July 19 and the institute opened October 20, 1939. Two large dormitories, a garage, barn, and workshop comprise the new Kentucky Mountain Bible Institute plant. Many of the graduates from the Mount Carmel High School enter here for the three-year college course. The Kentucky Mountain Bible Institute is the only educational institution in Breathitt County offering courses in Greek. College English, Theology, Homiletics, Missions, and kindred subjects are also a part of the curriculum in this school. Of the thirty-three young men and women who have graduated from the Kentucky Mountain Bible Institute, all but two have entered some field of church work, most of them now working in the mountains of eastern Kentucky.

MOUNT CARMEL CHURCH SCHOOL, a Class A high school, was founded in 1925 by Rev. Miss Lela G. McConnell. In August, 1924, Mr. and Mrs. J. B. Lawson deeded twelve acres of Mount Carmel's present tract as a site for a church and school. The first spadeful of ground was turned for the school building in March, 1925. Previous to this a neighborhood "working" had cleared the land of blacksnakes, sumac, underbrush, small trees, and briers. A dormitory for boys and the main building, a three-story frame structure with a stone and cement foundation, were completed and dedicated in September, 1925. In the summer of 1938 several new buildings were erected on the campus and an addition was made to the boys' dormitory. This doubled the capacity of the school.

In 1932 Mr. and Mrs. J. P. Crain gave twenty acres of land to the school. This gift enabled the school to add to its playgrounds a baseball diamond, two tennis courts, a basketball and volleyball court, and croquet grounds. A gas well, drilled on this land before the establishment of the school, was piped into the buildings when they were first erected. The well has a pressure of 250 pounds and supplies light, heat, and fuel for cooking. A cave, built into the side of a hill, provides storage for fruits and vegetables.

When the school opened for the first term there were five faculty members, all graduates of Asbury College, Wilmore, Kentucky, and fifty-eight students. The teaching standards of Pennsylvania and New Jersey were introduced into the curriculum of the school, which included Latin among its studies. During the 1938-39 school term 113 pupils were enrolled. Of this number fifty-two were boys, sixty-one girls, and sixty-five were boarding, and forty-eight day students. Some of the day students who walk around ten miles to and from school cross the Kentucky River (North Fork) three times in a boat to reach the school from their homes. Ten counties were represented in the 1939-40 enrollment of the school: Perry, Wolfe, Lee, Magoffin, Menifee, Morgan, Knott, Lester, Lewis, Breathitt, together with a few students from North Carolina and the Tennessee Mountains.

3. OAKDALE VOCATIONAL SCHOOL, ten miles west of Jackson by railroad, thirteen by a good-weather road, and thirty by the best road, is conducted by the Free Methodist Church. In 1920 Miss Elizabeth E. O'Connor, a Pennsylvania-born Free Methodist missionary, began teaching "readin', 'ritin', and 'rithmetic" in her home near Oakdale to some of the children in the neighborhoood. These small home-taught classes developed into a regular school and in 1922 a full-time grade school was opened in the Mission Church that had already been erected here. Ground was donated to the school in August, 1929, by Alex. Wilson, and in October the first spadeful of dirt was turned for the present Administration Building, a four-story frame structure.

The High School Department, added in 1930, graduated its first class in 1935. It is now accredited by the Kentucky State Association of Colleges and Secondary Schools as a Class A high school. The library, containing 1,700 volumes, is one of the best in the county. Oakdale has a faculty of eight members, and a total enrollment of 100 (1939-40). The school offers to those who do not wish to take the regular high school course a Certificate Course, which includes work in the Vocational Department and courses in religion. Like the other church schools in the county, the Oakdale Vocational School is a mission center.

The Home Arts Cottage, a one and one-half-story boxed building, is used by the home "ec" girls as a practice home. The shop, equipped with work tables, lathe, and tools provides training in general woodwork, metalwork, home mechanics, and broom-making. The institution is lighted and obtains power from an up-to-date Diesel plant. A forty-acre farm on the opposite side of the railroad tracks provides the school with much of its food.

4. HIGHLAND INSTITUTE, at Guerrant, fifteen miles from Jackson on the Highland-Athol Road (State 52), is the "Berea of Breathitt." The plant, spread out over a seven-acre campus, is picturesquely set in a lovely hill-encircled valley on the north side of Puncheon Camp Creek. The institution's 600-acre farm, donated by the Glendale College Club of Cincinnati as a Christmas present in 1937, extends for about three miles along the creek. The main or "Rock Building" is a two-story structure of gray sandstone, quarried on the school farm. The infirmary, located in this building, has a capacity of six beds and is the only other hospital in Breathitt County besides the Bach Memorial in Jackson. Until 1938-39 Highland had a resident physician whose place has now been taken by a registered nurse. The institution's infirmary serves the students, staff, and the surrounding community, and conducts a Mother and Baby Health Clinic.

In the furniture shop the boys receive training in various types of woodworking. Many of the things which they make are of practical value, such as hoghouses, gates, watering troughs, and chicken feeders. They also make bookshelves, magazine racks, and tool boxes. The shop turns out hand looms, bedroom and dining-room suites, coffee tables, nut bowls, plates, and other odds and ends for sale. This furniture, principally solid black walnut, is exhibited at the annual Harvest Festival at Quicksand and at other fairs during the year.

Students, by working a specific number of hours for their tuition and board, perform most of the varied work which most of them will follow. Some of them take care of the Holstein dairy herd, others take care of the poultry, hogs, and do other work on the farm. The practice-home for the girls is a seven-room building where the girls learn through experience every phase of the art of home-making. In this respect Highland is performing a much needed service towards better homes in the mountains. The cannery and laundry, housed together in a brick and tile building, and the saw- and gristmills also give Highland pupils opportunities to learn varied and efficient methods in these industries. The other buildings on the campus are of frame construction. These include a school building containing eight classrooms, a library, gymnasium, the principal's office, and a chapel.

Highland Institute offers the principal studies of elementary, junior and senior high schools with emphasis on practical training. In 1939-40 the total enrollment at Highland was 166; of these 63 were high school, 35 junior high, and 68 elementary students. Pupils come from Breathitt and near-by counties and from Virginia and Ohio. *The Highlander,* a school paper published here, has a circulation of 1,500.

The history of Highland is one of the chapters in the career of Dr. E. O. Guerrant. In May, 1907, after two visits to Puncheon Camp Creek, and in response to many requests, he located two teachers here. They took up their residence in a shack, and started a school under a sycamore that still stands on the Highland campus. On May 18, 1907, Dr. and Mrs. E. O. Guerrant and Judge William Beckner came to Puncheon Camp Creek, and with the assistance of Proctor Bill Little, Breck Herald, and others put up a large tent in which to preach the next day. Sunday morning, May 19, was a beautiful day. There was a large crowd by 9:00 A.M. when Dr. Guerrant preached a short sermon. Judge Beckner then spoke on the value of church education. They then took a subscription of $531 to build the college and a chapel. Dr. Guerrant added $500 for a Mr. Hughes and Mr. Brewer. Mr. Breck Herald gave four acres of his land, all the lumber for the college, coal, and $100.

The Used Clothing Department of Highland twice a week holds "sales" of the clothing sent to the institution. Farm produce, including vegetables of all kinds, chickens, eggs, and fruit is exchanged by people in this and neighboring communities for clothing of all kinds. Some of the Highland pupils do extra work for clothing which they receive from this department.

5. A CREVICED HILL, eighteen miles from Jackson near the confluence of Onion Pen Branch and Canoe Creek (Middle Fork) on the Hiram Sizemore place, is one of the most unusual natural phenomena in Breathitt County. Beneath the thin layer of soil on this tree-covered hill there is solid rock. At regular intervals this massive rock has been rent in circular lines around the hill. When pebbles are dropped into the deeply rent crevices, which appear to be straight down, their clink is heard after a short pause. The sound is that of a rock hitting tin or some other metal. Many people visit this place to see and hear this phenomenon.

6. MORRIS FORK, one of the larger and more progressive of Breathitt's many remote communities, is situated in the southwestern tip of the county, about ten miles from Canoe. The unimproved county road, passing through picturesque and idyllic country along the Middle Fork, can only be traveled in good weather when the water is low. It crosses the Middle Fork at Elsoms Creek and then, when it turns up Morris Fork, it crosses the creek bed several times. In bad weather and during high water traveling by horse- or muleback is the surest way of reaching Morris Fork. The community, named for the stream on which it is located, has an up-to-date county school with a large playground and with facilities for social programs and recreation. Rev. Samuel Vandermeer, a northern Presbyterian minister who vacationed here in 1924, remained and became a community leader. He and his wife, a trained nurse, have carried on a program of diversified activities which have set Morris Fork apart in spirit as well as in appearance from numerous other remote settlements in the mountains. The nine-room community center is an outgrowth of Rev. Mr. Vandermeer's work in this section. The small, belfried church, in Gothic style and of semirustic construction, is built of white oak covered with stained shingles on the outside and stained to match on the inside. Barkstripped logs support the beamed ceiling; and amber glass windows pleasingly blend with the rich brown color scheme of the church.

7. THE ROBINSON AGRICULTURAL EXPERIMENT SUBSTATION, with its headquarters and experimental farm at Quicksand, three miles southeast of Jackson on State 15, consists of 15,000 acres of land. This large tract, extending from the mouth of Quicksand Creek, a tributary of the North Fork, into neighboring Perry and Knott counties, was turned over to the University of Kentucky in 1922 by the late E. O. Robinson, of Fort Thomas, Kentucky, and the late F. W. Mowbray, of Cincinnati, Ohio, who for many years operated one of the largest lumber mills ever located in the Kentucky Mountains.

The substation was created by an act of the State Legislature in 1924, and funds are appropriated biennially for operating expenses. It is under the general supervision of the director of the Kentucky Agricultural Experiment Station, located at Lexington. The purpose of the substation is to carry on experiments and give demonstrations in reforestation and agriculture adapted to the region. Its work also includes horticulture and animal husbandry. A state forester, a home demonstrator, a superintendent, and a farm manager are among the regular employees.

On the farm there is a large orchard that includes every kind of tree bearing fruit in this climate, and a dairy of approximately twenty cows. Hogs are raised for breeding and are loaned out for this purpose throughout the region. The poorer types are butchered for market. Chickens and turkeys are also raised, and there is a demonstration cannery. The principal building of the substation is Cooper Hall, which is principally used for festival exhibits.

The Quicksand Harvest Festival, an agricultural, home-product fair for all of southeastern Kentucky, is held on the last Thursday and Friday of September. Since the first festival in 1926 it has become the biggest annual event in Breathitt County. In addition to regular farm exhibits in corn, field crops, stock, and poultry there are contests in ballad singing, folk dancing, string music, hog calling, chicken calling, and horseshoe pitching. Exhibits for women include breads, cakes, pies, candies, honey, molasses, cottage cheese, home-made soap, canned goods, and textiles such as bedcovers, rugs, house furnishings, and wearing apparel. There are special departments for school displays in sewing, weaving, and woodwork; and for 4-H Club exhibits in hogs, poultry, corn, potatoes, clothing, canning, and cooking. Another department includes antiques and Indian relics.

Thousands of people, old and young, come out from their isolated creek valley homes to attend the festival, many of the oldest ones leaving their community for the first time during the year. The half-forgotten styles of former years make their appearance along with spic-and-span jeans, freshly-ironed cotton dresses, overalls, and the latest creations of New York modistes. Stolid mountaineers with their retiring women, some with small babies in their arms, scrutinize the "goings on," and occasionally indulge their sly humor. "Mountain dew" contributes generously towards the carnival spirit. Music, song, and dance give it gusto and color. Several thousand mountain people move about greeting old friends and their innumerable relatives, renewing acquaintances and making new ones, talking of farm and home and other people.

8. DR. WILGUS BACH COLLECTION OF ANTIQUES, housed on the second floor of the Hiram Bach grocery at Stevenson, twelve miles from Jackson on State 30, contains old documents, Indian flints, clocks, guns, books, spinning wheels, reels, and other domestic objects. Among the time-stained documents is the original deed from Wylic Cope to John Back and his son Joseph, dated September 14, 1836, for approximately 33,000 acres of land on the Quicksand. Two thousand dollars in gold was exchanged in this transaction. Two other Bach documents, a marriage bond of 1812 and a deed for the lot upon which the Hargis Building in Jackson now stands, dated September 23, 1840, are also included in the collection. The lot was then sold to Isaac Back (*sic*) for $30. A yellowed piece of paper bearing the date 1848, and found in the strong box of Stephen Williams, Quicksand, carries the hocus-pocus of a witch doctor's prescription. At the bottom has been added: "'for good luck always put a small pinch of salt in the vessel before milking."

An old English catechism bought by Johann Christian Bach, in 1762, when he became chief musician in the Royal Palace in London, England, is one of the most valued articles in the collection. This catechism was later owned by Joseph Back and his wife, Elizabeth Huffman, who brought it into eastern Kentucky from Culpepper County, Virginia, in 1798. It has remained in the Bach family since its original purchase by Johann Christian Back, the son of Johann Sebastian, and the first to anglicize the spelling and pronunciation of the name by changing the "h" to "k."

An old Bible in this collection was traded by Spencer Adams, in 1801, to Stephen Hogg for a large tract of land above Whitesburg, Letcher County, Kentucky. It was given to his grandson, Judge James Back, provided he would read it through and he in turn gave it to his son, Lazarus W. P. Back, if he would read it through. Later it was given to Dr. Wilgus Bach.

The small gun collection contains two "long," or Kentucky rifles, better known locally as "hog" rifles. One of them is a flintlock and the other a cap and ball. A powder horn and pouch hangs near by from the deer's antlers or "bucks." In a glass case are flint rocks, a miscellaneous assortment of bones, two skulls, an elongated cannon ball, and a very old pistol.

There are two old clocks in this collection. One of them in a wooden cabinet six feet high is believed to be over a hundred years old. The other, a mantel type, is believed to be even older and is considered one of the early successors to the clocks made entirely of wooden parts.

There are several old cooking kettles of great depth, a pair of old firedogs, two steelyards (weighing instruments) at least 150 years old, an old wooden bread tray, gourds, four shuttles, an old milk pail known as a piggin, a surveying chain of the old type, and a last for making shoes.

The large loom in this collection, now somewhat rickety, is made of walnut. Three reels, used in measuring thread for making yarn and flax, "crack" every 100 complete turns. There are two spinning wheels, one small and the other large. Two boards, each with a square of nail-like projections through them, are known as hackles and were once used for taking sheals out of beaten flax.

9. NAILORS ROCK, about thirteen miles southwest of Jackson (seven miles on State 15), is a strikingly prominent pedestal at the head of the Little Fork of Canoe

and Howard's creeks. It covers almost a half acre, and from its base to its highest point it is approximately one hundred feet high. The gigantic rock, a particularly resistant sandstone outcropping, has split in several places from top to bottom. A large oak tree once stood on the top, according to the oldest inhabitants of the vicinity. While smaller, looser rocks, and sandy soils have been washed and worn away to lower levels, it has stood in massive defiance to the weathering agencies of nature. Erosion, however, has in many places contoured and smoothed its surfaces, designed fanciful and fantastic patterns, and given it the mellowed aspects of age. In the summer it is spotted with vegetation. At one place, where the rock has been sundered, there are projections which serve as steps in climbing up the rock. Near the top it comes together again, but at this point a small hole has been eroded through. The opening is rather small and a large person has to squeeze through. After getting through, one can easily climb upon the last rocky level. Nailors Rock is one of the most outstanding oddities of nature in Breathitt County. It is a picnic and party spot, and many people in this region visit it on Easter Sunday.

Nailors Rock, named for a Mr. Nailor, has a curious history. Almost a half century ago a man of this name came to Breathitt County in search of the half legendary silver mine or the buried treasures of John Swift. Every summer during the decade 1760-70 the fabulous Swift came through the mountains into Kentucky where, it is said, he worked a silver mine. Mr. Nailor brought with him maps and an instrument that many superstitiously believed could detect deposits or the presence of precious ore and metal. After prospecting about the county he started digging the shaft which may still be seen. He worked hard and patiently for many days. Then, after reaching a certain depth, he stopped and disappeared from the scene as suddenly as he had come upon it. The inhabitants in the vicinity never knew the outcome of his undertaking. He left behind the ladder which he used in his well and it remained there many years until it was finally obliterated by decay. Several years ago a company of Civilian Conservation Corps boys started laying the foundation for an observation tower on top of this rock. Upon their return one morning they found their work torn down, and the project was abandoned.

10. RIVERSIDE CHRISTIAN TRAINING SCHOOL, at Lost Creek on State 15, was founded in 1906 by Mr. and Mrs. G. E. Drushal who still head the school (1940). The three-acre campus is ideally situated on a rounded bottom at the confluence of Troublesome and Lost Creeks. Riverside today is an accredited school with the eight lower grades, a four-year high school, and a Bible department.

Shortly after the arrival, of the Drushals in 1906, the public school at Lost Creek ended its session. Pursuing their ideal of a church school "nestled among the hills where the Bible could be taught daily," they wrote letters, talked, and otherwise agitated for what shortly afterward became Riverside Institute. In the summer of 1906 three acres of land were purchased from Dan Cornett and a chapel with two classrooms and another building for a parsonage were soon under way.

For several years the school children of Riverside were mostly from Lost Creek although a few came from other districts and boarded with relatives. An extra teacher came in 1907 and boarded with the Drushals. One day, as plans were being made for the opening of another term of school, Henry B. Noble called at the parsonage and said he had five children he wanted to send to Riverside. The biggest room in the parsonage was curtained off into two rooms and given to them. Other buildings and additions were made after this to meet the needs of the school.

In 1931 Arthur Haddix and Beech Davidson donated some adjoining land and shortly thereafter three buildings were erected on the new tract. One of these was the present Administration Building known as "The Log House." The roof of this building is covered with handmade shingles. The other two buildings were dormitories, the larger and newer one being destroyed by fire in December, 1939. The Cicero Noble Gymnasium, named for the man who gave the first one hundred dollars for lumber, was built almost entirely by student labor. The instiute's first school building, enlarged by four more rooms, has been rented by the Breathitt County Board of Education since 1916, and today it houses the Lost Creek Consolidated School.

Educational work is considered only a byproduct of the religious work which the institution as a missionary center conducts. The present (1939-40) faculty consists of a superintendent, one grade teacher, four high school teachers, and a Bible teacher. Students who came principally from near-by mountain counties, with a few from other states, work on the 115-acre school farm to help defray the expenses of their tuition and board.

In 1931 Riverside, founded and more widely known as "Institute," was incorporated under the name of "Riverside Christian Training School," with a board of trustees as its governing body.

11. CLAYHOLE (170 pop., 850 alt.), on Troublesome Creek, twelve miles south from Jackson, on State 15, now a peaceful community, flared into the newspaper headlines of the Nation on November 8, 1921, as the scene of an election-day massacre. Clayhole precinct, a stronghold of one of the two major political parties, was considered a key to the outcome of the election in Breathitt. According to one version, the events that led up to the "battle" had been planned. The rumor was spread the night before that the polling place would be "torn up" when it was opened in the morning. The fact that the phone lines were cut strengthened the belief that men were organized to carry on a fight.

The battle occurred shortly after the polls were opened. A candidate for the office of county judge, defeated in the August, 1921, primary, was said to have led a party of men to the voting place and demanded a fair election after a voter had been challenged. He was asked to leave the room and remove his men from the door. Upon refusing, election officers attempted to remove him by force. Without warning or threat, scores of shots were fired. When the gunfire stopped, men were lying about the polling place, some dead and others dying. The election clerk was the first to fall. His wife, who appeared in time to see her husband slain, knocked the pistol from the hand of the man she said shot him. At the end of the fusillade four men had been killed and eight were wounded inside the polling place and around its door.

The second and more reliable version of this bloody incident attributed it to a mix-up and dispute between two clerks of the election, for whom there were conflicting authorizations. A clerk had already been certified by the Breathitt County election commissioners when, on the day before election, a second party came before them and made affidavit that the clerk they had previously certified was ill and could not serve. He requested that the ballot box be turned over to him. The trouble started, according to this explanation, when the clerk first authorized appeared at the polls and demanded to serve. Upon subsequent investigation, however, it was found that the difference between the two clerks had been settled before the fighting began.

Efforts were made to reopen the polls after the fight, but it was found the ballots had been thrown into the creek and few of them could be used. Few persons were daring enough to approach the polls after the battle. Physicians from Jackson hurried to the scene of the battle on a special train from the Mowbray and Robinson lumber plant at Quicksand.

During this same election, incidents in which gunfire played a part also occurred at the Simpson, Buckhorn, and Spring Fork precincts. At the end of this tragic election day around a dozen men had been shot to death and many had been wounded.

12. FLINT MOUNTAIN, one of the largest ridges shedding water between Troublesome and South Quicksand and their tributary creeks, is most easily approached by an unimproved county road leading up Russell Branch. Until the period of white settlement in this region, this mountain was visited by Indians who found here in profusion the flint from which it took its name.

PART III. APPENDIX

GENERAL INDEX

Acreage, Breathitt County, 12
Adams, Samuel, 36
Adams, Spencer, 146
Agricultural Department, Breathitt County High School, 114
Agricultural Experiment Substation (Quicksand), 144-45
Agricultural "side lines" (industries), 15-16
Agricultural statistics, 12-15; 1840 census, 16
Agriculture, 12-17
Aikman, Big John, 62-63, 65, 66; sent to penitentiary, 69; ambushes Capt. Bill Strong, 75-76
Aikman, Dan, 56-57
Aikmans, The, 46
Airport (Jackson), 97; see also General Information
Allen, J. C. B. (Whick), justice of the peace, 62, 65, 66, 67
Allen, Samuel, 44
Allen, William, 50, 51
Allens, The, 47, 65
Alliance for Guidance for Rural Youth, 112
Altitudes, see Elevations
Ambush in the mountain feuds, 55, 59, 74, 75, 76; see also Assassinations
Amis, John, killed, 58
Amis, Capt. Thomas, 57-58
Amis, Wiley, 57
Amis', The, 46, 47
Amusements, xiii
Anderson, Chris, 23
Anderson, Myrtle, vii
Annual events, xiii
Antiques: Dr. Wilgus Bach collection of, 145-46; at Quicksand Harvest Festival, 145
Arlington Hotel, 91
Arrowood, Bertha, vii
Arrowood, Rev. Nathan, 119

Arrowoods, The, 46
Art Department, Breathitt County High School, 113-14; exhibits, 114
Ashford, S. P., 105
Assassinations: Curtis Jett, Jr., 59; Logan Cockrell, 60; Judge John Wesley Burnett and Tom Little, 67; J. B. Marcum, 94, 127; Ed Callahan, 78; see also Ambush, Daniel Freeman, and James Deaton

Baby and Mother Health Clinic (Highland Institute), 141
Bach, see also Back. (These spellings often used interchangeably by the members of this family.)
Bach, Farish, 110
Bach, Hiram, vii, 128, 145
Bach, Johann Sebastian, 146
Bach Memorial Hospital, 96, 128
Bach, Miles, 102
Bach, Dr. Wilgus, 128; collection of antiques, 145-146
Bachs, The, 47, 145-46
Back, see also Bach. (These spellings are often used interchangeably by the members of this family.)
Back, Grannis, vii
Back, Elizabeth Huffman, 146
Back Hotel, 95
Back, Isaac, 84, 145
Back, Deputy Sheriff James, 60, 66
Back, Judge James, 60, 66, 146
Back, Johann Christian, 145, 146
Back, John, 145
Back, Joseph, 145, 146
Back, Lazarus W. P., 146
Back, William D., 90

154 *BREATHITT*

Bakers, The, 46
Ballad singing, 144
Barker, Rev. T. W., 95
Banks', The, 47
Baptist Churches, see Churches (denominations), and Church Buildings
Barkley Bowl (stadium), 97, 131
Bays, The, 47
Becknells, The, 46
Beckner, Judge William, 142
Bees and bee gums, 16
Beginning Branch School, 103-4
Bell, U. R., viii
"Berea of Breathitt," 141, see Highland Institute
Big Rock Consolidated School, 112
Biggerstaff, "Uncle Ben," 122
Birchfield, Adams, 36
Blanton, Mrs. Dora, 110
"Bloody Breathitt," appellation, 6
"Bloody Bucket, The" (Jackson), 136
Bluegrass and Rhododendron (John Fox, Jr.), 30
Bohanon, Louis C., 25
Bohanon, Simon, first county court clerk, 50, 85
Bohanons, The, 47
Bollings, The, 46
Boone, Daniel, 36
Bowman, Col. Abraham, 128
Brashear(s), Colonel Robert F., salt works, 25, 29
Breathitt County: establishment of, 48-50; county's namesake, 52; location of county seat, 49-50; county, circuit and fiscal courts, 50, 64, 93; county jail, 27, 50, 74, 128; board of education, 148; county offices in Federal Bldg., 135; distinction in World War I, 3; see Courthouse, Court clerks office building, *and* entries under County
B r e a t h i t t County Citizens Bank, 93
Breathitt County High School: b u i l d i n g, facilities and grounds, 132; curriculum and depts., 112-14, 132; dedicated (1939) by Mrs. Franklin D. Roosevelt, 132; see *also* School Enrollments
"Breathitt County pistols," 70
Breathitt, Gov. John, county's namesake, 52
Breathitt Town, name changed to Jackson (1845), 50, 51, 84
Breathitt, William, 52
Breathitt's first and only legal hanging, 91-93
Brethren Church, see United Brethren in Christ
Bridges (Jackson): 93; swinging bridge, 97
Brickmaking (Jackson), 89
Brittain, Nathan, 128
B r y a n t, W i l l i a m, deputy sheriff, 92
Bryants, The, 46
Buckhorn Creek School, 111
Bullock, James M., 50
Buncombe County (N. C.) Baptist Church, 119
Burnett, Judge John Wesley, 61-63; elected judge, 62, 66; assassinated, 67
Bushwhacking, 56, 70, 87
Bus lines, xiii
Butler, Judge D. K., 61, 62

Callahan (Ed)-Deaton Rivalry, 71-73
Callahan, Ed, 70-75; assassinated, 76
Callahan, Jerry, 57
Callahan-Marcum-Hargis-Cockrell feud, 76
Callahan-Strong feud, 70-76
Callahan, Wilson, 57-58, 70
Callahans, The, 46
Campbell, Lewis, 119
Campbells, The, 47
Caney Consolidated School, 111
Cannel coal, 18; largest block ever mined, 19, 20
Cardwell, John, 47, 85
Cardwell, J. W., 89
Cardwell, Thomas P., 47
Cardwells, The, 46, 47
Carpenter, "Uncle Steve," 107
Carpenters, The, 47

Catholics, none in Breathitt, 123
Cattle and other livestock, 13; feeding of, 15
"Cattle War," 58
Census, see Population, General Information, also School census, and Agricultural statistics
Centers, Herman, 90
Central University, 109, 130, 131
Chandler, Samuel P., 119
Chandlers, The, 47
Chapman, George, 101
Chesapeake & Ohio Railroad, 33, 87
Cheves, Capt. R. S., editor, *Mt. Sterling Democrat,* 68
Christian Church, see Church Buildings, and Churches (denominations)
Christmas in Jackson, 81, 91
Church buildings: all denominations ("Liberty" Church), 119; Baptist — on Quicksand, 117, on Middle Fork (Canoe), 119, at Jackson (Missionary), 95, 96, Primitive), 110; Methodist—119, ("Free"), 122-23, at Jackson, 87, 95; Christian—Hazel Green (Wolfe County), 119, 120, at Jackson, 95; Presbyterian — Day's, 121, Jett's Creek, 121, 124, at Jackson, 89, 95, 96; United Brethren in Christ (Lost Creek), 122, 148
Church schools: in the education of the county, 108-9; see separate entries for Lees Junior College, Highland Institute, Kentucky Mountain Bible Institute, Mount Carmel Church School, Oakdale Vocational School, and Riverside Christian Training Institute
Churches (denominations): Baptist—(Hard-Shell, Regular, Primitive), 117-18, at Jackson, 110, (Missionary) at Jackson, 95; Christian—119-20, at Jackson, 95; Methodist—117, at Jackson, 87, 95, ("Free"), 122; United Brethren in Christ, 122, 148; Presbyterian—117, 123, 124, at Jackson, 89, 95, 96
Clark, Gov. James, 49, 50
Clark, Capt. Jonathan, 128
Clayhole "Massacre," 149-50
Clayhole (Combs) School, 105, 111
Clothing exchanged for farm produce (Highland Institute), 142
Clubs: 4-H, 17, 145; F.F.A., 17, 114-15
Coal mines and mining, 17-20
Cockrell, Evaline, 62
Cockrell, James, 59
Cockrell, John, 120
Cockrell-Hargis-Marcum-Callahan feud, 76
Cockrell, Logan, killed, 60
Cockrell, "Aunt Milly," 120
Cockrell, Millie, 49
Cockrell, Simon, Sr., 48, 49, 50, 84
Cockrell Subscription School, 99-100
Cockrell, William, 99, 100
Cockrells, The, 47, 94
Collections of antiques: Bach at Stevenson, 145-146; at Quicksand Harvest Festival, 145
Collegiate Institute (S. P. Lees) at Jackson, see Lees Junior College
Collins, L. and R. H., *History of Kentucky,* 86
Colomba (Prosper Merimee), 53
Combs, Annabelle, vii
Combs, "Old" Bill, 86
Combs, Breck, high sheriff, 92
Combs, George, 45
Combs, Hagins, and Patrick, 90
Combs, Hardin, 50
Combs, Harrison, 44, 45, 101
Combs, Henry, 45-46, 101
Combs Hotel, 95
Combs, Hugh, 45
Combs, Matthew, 44, 45
Combs, Capt. N. B., 90
Combs, Steve, 45

156 *BREATHITT*

Combs Subscription School, 101
Combs, William, 74
Combs, W. M., 104
Combs', The, 47
Community Center (Morris Fork), 143
Community Playground (Jackson), 97, 131
Consolidated County Schools, 111-12
Convention days (county), Democratic, 71
Cooper Hall (Quicksand Agricultural substation), 144
Cope, Wylie, 145
Copeland Station Salt Works, 26
Cope, Capt. A. C., vii
Cope, James P., 50
Cope, Tom, vii
Copes, The, 47, 118
Cornett, Dan, 148
Corsican vendettas, 53
County agricultural agent, 135
County Courthouse, *see* Courthouse
County Government, early, 50-52
County Health Board, 135
County Jail, 128
County's namesake, 52
County and subscription schools: first, 99; Beginning Branch, 103, 104; Big Rock, 111-12; Buckhorn Creek, 103, 111-12; Caney, 111-12; Clayhole, 105; Cockrell, 99-100; Combs, 101, 105; Elkatawa, 108; Fugate's Fork, 111-12; Haddix, 111-12; Haddix Fork, 111-12; Hardshell, 111-12; Jett, 102; Lost Creek, 111-12; Meetin'-house, 102-103; Miller's, 103; Mouth of Loveless Branch, 102; Mouth of Old Buck, 103; Puncheon Camp Creek, 108; Quicksand, 102; Round Bottom, 102; Spring Fork, 107; Vancleve, 111-12; Wilhurst, 111-12; *see also* Church Schools and Jackson Schools
County seat: first location (Quicksand) 49; changed to Jackson, 50

Court clerks' office building, 86-87; burned, 87; 88
Court records destroyed, 58, 87, 102, 127
Court rooms, Federal Building (Jackson), 135
Courthouse: charter provision, 50; log, 86; taken over by Capt. Strong, 59-60; brick, 86-87; described, 88, 89; present (1941), 127
Courthouse Square, 78, 91, 127, 128
"Court-martials" (Strong's), 58
Covey, Rev. Nixon, 85, 120
Crafts, The, 47
Crain Hotel, 95
Crain, Mr. and Mrs. J. P., 139
Crain, M. S., 136
Crawford, A. D., store, 94
Crawford, Archibald, 32
Crawford, Claiborn, 50
Crawfords, The, 46, 47
Creviced Hill (Onion Pen Branch and Canoe Creek), 143
Crops, *see* Agriculture
Cumberland Gap, 35
Curricula: of early schools, 106-7, 111; of all church schools, 109; Breathitt High, 112-15, 132; Highland Institute, 141-43; Kentucky Mountain Bible Institute, 139; Mount Carmel Church School, 140; Oakdale Vocational School, 140-41; Riverside Institute, 149
Cutoff (Jackson), The, 82, 132-33, 135

Daniels, Dr. K. B., vii
Davidson, Beech, 148
Davis, R. T., coal mine, 17
Davis, William, 85
Day Brothers Lumber Company, 24
Day Brothers store, 94
Day log booms at Jackson, 23-24
Day, William, Sr., 121
Days, The, 47

GENERAL INDEX 157

"Death of Many, The" (rifle), 74
Deaton, Bob, 73
Deaton-Callahan Rivalry, 71-73
Deaton, James, 71-72; killed, 73
Deatons, The, 47, 72
Democratic (County) convention days, 71
Denominations, see Churches (denominations)
Depot at Jackson, 95
Dickey, Rev. John Jay, 87, 89, 90, 108-9, 122, 129, 130
Dodge, William E., 130
Donoho, David, vii, viii, 113
Draft quota, filled by volunteers (World War I), 3
Drushal, Mr. and Mrs. G. E., vii, 109, 122, 148
Duffs, The, 47

Early county government, 50-52
Early feuds of "Bloody Breathitt," 53-76
Early salt works, 25-26
Eastern Kentucky Hardwood Company, 24
Economic development of Breathitt, 12-33
Education, 99-116
Election-day massacre (Clayhole), 149-50
Elections of 1878 (Little-Burnett feud), 61-63
Elevations, 11
Elkatawa Subscription School, 108
Elkbutt Knob, elevation, 11
Eskippakithiki, 34
Establishment of Breathitt County, 48-50
Evans', The, 46
Eve, Judge Joseph, 51
Events, annual, xiii
Ewen Hotel, 95
Experiment substation, Robinson Agricultural, 144-45

Fairs: Jackson School, xiii; Quicksand, 144-45
Falls of the Ohio, 34
Farm produce exchanged for clothing (Highland Institute), 142
Farming, see Agriculture
"Father of Breathitt County, The," 49
Federal Building (Jackson), 96; history, description, offices, 135
Federal Work Relief, 97, 111, 128, 131
Feltner, J. C., vii
Feuds of "Bloody Breathitt": Callahan-Strong, 70-71, 73-76; Deaton-Callahan, 71-74; bushwhacking and guerilla bands, 56, 70, 87; Little-Burnett, 61-63; Little-Jett, 59-61; Strong-Amis, 58; general background and origin, 54-55, 56; general pattern, 55-56; economic motivation, 6; logging operations, 23, 72; dying feud spirit, 76
Finley, John, 34
"Firing-squad," Strong's, 74
First brick house in Jackson, 87
First Explorations of Kentucky (J. Stoddard Johnston), 35
First "Military Occupation" (Jackson), 59-60
First motion picture (Jackson), 95
First National Bank (Jackson), 93
First Negro school (1867), 104
First and Only Legal Hanging Breathitt County), 91-93
First Presbyterian Church (Louisville), 121
First settlers, 39-47
First travelers, 34-38
Fish, xiii
Fletcher, Mr. and Mrs. Fred, 139
Flinchum, David, kills a Negro, 59
Flinchums join the Cockrells (feud), 59
Flinchums, The, 47
Flint Mountain, 150
Flora, 137-38
Folk Dancing, 144
(Four) 4-H Clubs, 17, 145

Fox, John, Jr., author, on rafting, 30; treatment of feuds, 53
Fox, Tom, 51
Frazier, Thomas J., 85
Fraziers, The, 47
Free Methodist Church, 122-23, 140
Freeman, Daniel, killed, 65
Freeman, William, 65
French-Eversole feud (Petty County), 92
"Frog" Schools, 99
Frozen Creek, origin of name, 36
Frozen Creek pioneer settlers, 47
Frozen Mountain, elevations 11; point of interest, 137-38
Fugate's Fork School, 111
Furniture Shop (Highland Institute), 141
Future Farmers of America (F. F. A.), 17, 114-15

Gabbards, The, 46
Gamble, Alfred, 67
Gambles, The, 65
Game, xiii
Garrard salt works, 25
Gas, 26-27; geological map of county, 27
Gay, Henry, 27-28
Geological map of Breathitt (1927), 27
Geological Survey (1854-55), on coal, 19
German or Dutch pioneer settlers, 47
Gillum, Mrs. O. J., vii
Ginseng, 15-16
Gist, Christopher, 12, 34, 35-36
Glendale College Club (Cincinnati), 141
Goff, John, 90-91
Goff, John, Jr., 88
Government, early county, 50-52
Griffing, James B., 85
Griffing, William, 85
Griffiths, The, 46
Gristmill (Highland Institute), 142
Gross, Jordon, 84

Guerrant, 103
Guerrant Dr. E. O., 95, 109, 120-22, 142
Guerrant Memorial Presbyterian Church (Jackson), 95
Guerrilla bands start feuds, 87
Gymnasiums: Breathitt County High School (auditorium), 132; Cicero Noble (Riverside Institute), 148; Highland Institute, 142; Jackson City High School, 131; Lees Junior College, 129

Haddix: hamlet, 25; salt works, 25-26
Haddix, Arthur, 148
Haddix coal mines, 18, 20
Haddix Fork School, 111-12
Haddix Hotel, 95
Haddixes, The, 47
Haddix, Col. John, 29, 31
Haddix, Samuel, 44
Haddix, Tom, vii, 16, 19, 26
Haddix, William, 25
Haddix, Wm. G., 19
Hagins, Daniel, 47
Hagins, Sheriff John Linville, 60, 63, 64, 66, 68, 69, 102
Hagins, Thomas, 46, 50, 85 (Also spelled Hagin and less frequently Higgins.)
Hagins, William, 46, 47
Hagins', The, 46
Halloween, in Jackson, 80-81; 1913 fire, 95, 96
Hamilton, LaMar, vii, viii
Hanging, Breathitt's first and only legal, 91-93; of Kilburn and Negro, 75
"Hard-shell" Baptists, see Church Buildings, and Churches (denominations)
Hard-shell School, 111
Hargis, Senator A. H., vii, 103
Hargis Bank Building, 67, 84, 145
"Hargis Bottoms" (Jackson), 132
Hargis Brothers, 17
Hargis-Cockrell-Marcum-Callahan Feud, 76
Hargis Commercial Bank, 93
Hargis, Mrs. Evaline, 110

GENERAL INDEX 159

Hargis, John S., first circuit court clerk, 50, 51, 84, 85, 88, 110
Hargis', The, 47
Harris, Henderson, 51
Harvest Festival (Quicksand), 114, 141, 144
Harveys, The, 47
Hatcher, Dr. O. Latham, 112
Hattons, The, 47
Hays, John, 85
Hays, Nick, 49
Hays', The, 47
Health Clinic, Mother and Baby (Highland Institute), 141
Hemp and flax, 14
Herald, Alexander, 50
Herald, Breck, 142
Heralds, The, 46
Higgins, Thomas, 50; see also Hagins
High schools, see Breathitt County High School, Church Schools, and Jackson schools
Highknob, 10; elevation, 11
Highland Institute: 103, 109, 121, 141-43
Highlander, The (Highland Institute), 142
Highways, 8, 32; see also General Information
Hippodrome (Jackson), 96
History of Kentucky, (Collins, L. and R. H.), 86; (Z. F. Smith), 105
Hogg, Stephen, 146
Hogs and cattle, 13
Hollan (Holland), Levi, 47
Home Arts Cottage (Oakdale), 141
Home demonstrator, 144
"Home Guard," see Guerrillas, Bushwhacking, and Feuds
Hospitals: Bach Memorial, 96, 128, 141; Highland Institute, 141
Hotel Ewen, 95
Hotel Jefferson, 95
Hotels of the past: earliest at Jackson, 84; later, 95
Howards, The, 47
Hurst, Herman (Harman), 44, 50
Hurst, R. A., 96

Hurst, Capt. W. L., 869
Hursts, The, 47
Hutsons, The, 47
Indian Old Fields, 34
"Indian Postoffice" (Jackson), 133
Infirmary (Highland Institute, 141

Jackson: history, 84-98; contemporary scene, 77-83; founded as county seat, 49; incorporated (1890), 88; first military occupation, 59-60; first brick house, 87; first motion picture, 95; brickmaking at, 89; public utilities, 97; Halloween fire, 95, 96; rafting from Jackson, 30; see Points of Interest in Jackson and Environs, Jackson Schools, County Seat, Church Buildings, and Churches (denominations)
Jackson Academy, see Lees Junior College
Jackson, President Andrew, 85
Jackson Chapter Sons of the American Revolution, 127-28
Jackson Collegiate Institute, see Lees Junior College
Jackson Deposit Bank, 93
Jackson points of interest, 127-36
Jackson Hustler, The, 20, 21, 23, 30, 44, 88, 89, 90, 122
Jackson School Fair, 80
Jackson schools: old school house, 88; new building, 95; high school building, 97; description of grade and high school buildings, 131; summary, 109-11; city school board, 104, 109-11; see also Breathitt County High School, and Lees Junior College
Jackson Times, The, 87, 106
Jackson, York M., vii
Jail, county, 50
Jefferson County Jail, 69
Jefferson Hotel, 95
Jett, Curtis, killed, 59, 102
Jett, Curtis, Sr., 59

160 *BREATHITT*

Jett, Hiram, shoots Jerry Little, 59, 60
Jett School, 102
Jett, Stephen, Jr., 102
Jett, Stephen, 46, 50
Jetts, The, 46
Jetts and Cockrells combine against the Littles, 59
Jews, none in Breathitt, 123
Johnson, Elkanah, 118
Johnson, Frank, 46
Johnson, Israel, 46
Johnson, James, 46
Johnsons, The, 46, 47
Johnston, J. Stoddard, author, 35
Jones, Maj. R. W., vii
Josephs, The, 47

Kashes, The, 47
Keiths, The, 47
Kentucky Geological (Coal) Survey, 19
Kentucky Mountain Bible Institute (Mount Carmel), 109, 138-39
Kentucky Union Land Company, 24
Kentucky Union Railroad, 32-33, 87, 89
Kentucky and West Virginia Power and Light Company, 97
Kentucky's Famous Feuds and Tragedies (C. G. Mutzenberg), 76
Kephart, Horace, author, 56
Kilburn, Hen, gunman, 65, 74; hanging of with a Negro, 75, 127
Kiwanis Club (Jackson), 80
Ku-Klux, 70, 73, 74, 75

Lackey, Alexander, 49
Land area (acreage) of Breathitt, 12
Landrum, Clyde D., vii
Landrum, Rev. R. W., 119
Langley, J. W. (U. S. Senator), 135
Lawson, Mr. and Mrs. J. B., 139
Leatherwood salt works, 25-26
Lees Junior College: 87, 89, 96, 108-9, 122, 128-31

Lees, Mrs. Susan P., 130
Lexington & Eastern Railroad Company, 33, 87
"Liberty" Church, 119
Libraries: Breathitt County, 97; Highland Institute, 142; Jackson City High School, 131; Lees Junior College, 129; Oakdale Vocational School, 140
Life Among the Hills and Mountains of Kentucky (W. R. Thomas), 55
Lilly, Col. H. C., 57
Lindon, Judge James, elected county judge, 69
Little, Alfred, 65, 67
Little-Burnett feud, 61-63-69
Little, Miss Cappie, 111
Little, Charles Jefferson, deputy sheriff, 64, 65; elected sheriff, 69; 87, 90, 135
Little, Jason: disinterment of wife, 63-64; charged with murder, 63, 66; returned to Jackson, 66, 67, 69; found guilty of murder, 69
Little, Jerry, kills Curtis Jett, Jr., is badly wounded, 59, 60, 61, 63, 67
Little-Jett feud, 59-62
Little Pict Town, 34
Little, Proctor Bill, 142
Little, Tom, assassinated, 67, 68
Littles, The, 46, 65
Livestock, *see* Agriculture
"Log-run," 23-24
Log stealing, 23; feud logging operations, 72
Logging, 21-24
Lost Creek salt works, 26
Lost Creek Consolidated School, 111, 149
Lost Creek pioneer settlers, 47
Louisville & Nashville Railroad, 33, 94
Loyal Land Company, 35

McAfee Brothers (George, James and Robert), 36-37
McConnell, Rev. Lela G., vii, 109, 123, 139
McCormack Chapel, 110

GENERAL INDEX 161

McCormack, Mrs. Cyrus H., 130
McCoun, James, Jr., 36
McCreary, Governor, 68
McIntosh, Steve, 65
McQuinn, Alex, 44
McQuinn, Mrs. Catherine, 92
McQuinns, The, 47
Manns, The 9, 47
Marcum-Callahan-Hargis-Cockrell feud, 76
Marcum, Edward, 69
Marcum Hotel, 95
Marcum, James B., U. S. Commissioner, 69, 72, 76; assassinated, 94, 127
Marcum, Ned, 63
Marker (Jackson), S. A. R., 127
Massacre (Clayhole), election-day, 149-50
Meeting-house School, 102-3
"Meetin's," 5-6
Merimee, Prosper (*Colomba*), 53
Methodist Church, see Church Buildings, and Churches (denominations)
Midcalf, Jacob, 119
Middle Fork pioneer settlers, 46
Miller, George, 103
Miller's Schoolhouse, 103
Millers, The, 47
Military occupation of Jackson, first, 59-60
Missionary Baptist Church, see Church Buildings and Churches (denominations)
"Missionary" Schools, see Church schools
"Mob Law" in Jackson, 67-68
Moore, Allen, 21, 22, 50
Moore, Daniel, 21, 22
Moore, James L., 110-11
Moores, The, 47
Morgan, John Hunt, 120
Morris Fork, 111, 124, 143
Mother and Baby Health Clinic (Highland Institute), 141
Mount Carmel Church School, 109, 123, 138, 139-40
Mt. Sterling Democrat, 68
Mountain Association (Baptist), 119

Mountain Bible Institute, Kentucky, 109, 138-39
Mouth of Loveless Branch Subscription School, 102
Mouth of Old Buck School, 103
Mowbray, F. W., 144
Mowbray and Robinson, 24, 150
Mulens', The, 47
Mutzenberg, C. G., author, 76

Nailorsrock, 146-48
Natural gas: 26; first piped into Jackson, 26-27, 97
Natural resources, 12-33
Neace, Austin, 41, 42-43, 44
Neace, Henry, 41
Neace, Jake, 44
Neace, Malinda (Allen), 41, 44
Neaces, The, 41-44, 47
Negro schools: first (1867), 104; (1940), 104
Nickell, Rev. Joseph, 119
Noble, Mrs. Cora, 110
Noble, Elijah, 110
Noble, Enoch, 41, 42, 43
Noble, Granville Pearl, 100
Noble Gymnasium, 148
Noble, Henry B., 148
Noble, James, 16
Noble, Jerry, 110
Noble, Nathan, 16, 41, 42, 43
Noble salt works, 26
Noble, Virginia (Neace), 41
Noble, William, 41, 42
Nobles, The, 41-44, 47
North Fork pioneer settlers, 47

Oakdale Vocational School: 102, 109, 140-41
O'Connor, Miss Elizabeth E., vii, 109, 122, 140
Ohio & Kentucky Railroad, 33
Ohio Land Company, 35
Oil, 26-27; map, 27
Our Southern Highlanders (Horace Kephart), 56

Panbowl, see Panhandle and Panbowl
Panbowl Branch pioneer settlers, 46
Panhandle mill, 134

Panhandle and Panbowl, 10, 132-35, 137
Panhandle Tunnel, 82, 133-34
Parsons, Dr., 85
Patrick, Alexander, 85
Patrick Hotel, 95
Patrick, John, viii
Patrick, John E., 90, 136
Patrick, Miss Katie, 90
Pattons, The, 47
Pelfreys, The, 47
Pence, Andrew, 50
Petroleum, 27
Points of interest in the county, 137-50
Points of interest in Jackson and environs, 127-36
Pollard, O. H., 94
Polly, Grandvill, a pauper, 127
Population: Jackson—(1870), 86; (1940), xiii; N e g r o (1870), 104; (1930), 104
Post Office (Jackson), see Federal Building
Potatoes, 14
Pound Gap, 34, 35, 36
Pratice Home for Girls: Oakdale, 141; Highland Institute, 142
P r e s b y t e r i a n Church, see Church B u i l d i n g s, and Churches (denominations)
Presbyterian Church (First) Louisville, 121
Presbyterian Missions in the S o u t h e r n United States (Ernest Trice Thompson), 120
Price, Gabriel W., 49
Primitive Baptist Church, see Church B u i l d i n g s and Churches (denominations)
Puncheon Camp Creek School, 108
Push-boats, 28-29

Quicksand Creek Subscription School, 102
Quicksand coal mines, 18
Quicksand (first) County High School, 132
Quicksand Harvest Festival, xiii, 114, 141, 144-45
Quicksand pioneer settlers, 47
Quicksand, Robinson Agricultural Experiment Substation, at, 144-45

Rader, Dr. J. E., murder of, 91-93
Railroads: xiii, 32-33, 87-89, 91, 97
Randall, Judge William, 64, 65, 68
Rawlings, Jack, 136
Recollections of Breathitt (J. Green Trimble), 31-32, 51, 85, 99, 118,
Recreations, xiii
Religion, 117-24; see Church Buildings and Churches (denominations)
Redwine, Judge David B., 94
"Regular" Baptist Church, see Church B u i l d i n g s and Churches (denominations)
Religious background of settlers, 117
Rice, George, 89
Richeys, The, 47
Riffle, Frank, viii
Riverside Christian Training School (Riverside Institute, Lost Creek), 109, 111, 122, 148-49
Riverside Hotel, 90, 95
Roads, xiii, 8, 32
Roberts', The, 47
Robinson Agricultural Experiment Substation, 144-45
Robinson, E. O., 144
Robinson and Mowbray, 24, 144
R o b i n s o n (Stuart), School (Letcher County), 121
Rock Houses, 10, 133
Roosevelt, Mrs. Franklin D., dedicates B r e a t h i t t High School, 132
Round Bottom coal mines (Quicksand), 18
Round Bottom School, 102
Rowland, Mr., 88
Russells, The, 47
Ryland, W. E., 90

Salaries of Early School Teachers, 100, 109, 110, 111
Salt works, 25-26
Sandstone, 26-27

GENERAL INDEX 163

Sawmill (Highland Institute), 142
Sawmills, 21-24
Searcy, Miss Anna, 102
School attendance, *see* School census
School building statistics, county schools: (1880), 107; (1893), 107-108; (1900), 108; (1900-11), 108; (1932), 111; (1940), 111; *see also* School Districts
School census: (1851-60), 103-104; (1852), 104; (1862), 104; (1866), 104; Negro (1867), 104; (1869), 104; (1899-1900), 107; (1911), 107; (1940), 109; effect of cropping on attendance, 106; *see* School Enrollments
School Districts: (1851-67), 103-4; Negro (1867), 103-4; (1869), 104; (1899-1900), 107; (1911), 107-108; (1940), 111
School enrollment: all private schools, 109; total high school enrollment, 116; high school enrollment in church schools, 109; Breathitt County High School (1927, 1937-38, 1938-39), 132; Jackson City High and Grade School (1938-39), 131; Highland Institute (1939-40), 142; Lees Junior College (1938-39), 131; Kentucky Mountain Bible Institute, 139; Mount Carmel Church School (1938-39), 140; Oakdale Vocational School (1939-40), 140; Riverside Institute (1938-39), 131
School Fair, Jackson, xiii
"School-keepin," 104
Schools, *see* Church schools, County and subscription schools, and Jackson schools
Scotch border wars, 53
Sebastians, The, 46
Settlers, first, 39-47; later, 46-47
Settlement in the Cumberland foothills, 39-41
Sewell, Benjamin, 84
Sewell, Fanny, 84
Sewell, George W., 67, 129
Sewell, H. Price, viii
Sewell, John, 85
Sewell, Thomas, 84, 85
Sewell, William, 84
Sewells, The, 47
Shackelfords, The, 47
Sheffields, The, 47
Shockeys, The, 47
Shooting-match, an old-fashioned, 135
Sizemore, Hiram, 143
Smith, Arch, viii
Smith, "Bad" Tom, 91-93
Smith, "Raccoon" John, 119-20
Smith, Z. F., author, 105
Snake Valley (Jackson), 136
Snowden, J. M., 90
Social life in Jackson, 79
Sons of the American Revolution, Jackson Chapter, 127-28
"Sounding" (Pound) Gap, 34
South Jackson, 82; airport, 9
South, Jeremiah (Jerry), Father of Breathitt County, 49, 50, 84, 85
South, Richard, 50
Southern Mountain Workers' Regional Conference, 112
Southern Women's Educational Alliance, 112
Souths, The, 47
Spicer's Branch coal mine, 19
Speedsmith, John, 49
Spencers, The, 47
Spicer's Branch Coal Mine, 19
Spicers, The, 46; Spicer farm, 121
Spring Fork Creek settlers, 46
Spurlock, Jesse, 85
Spurlocks, The, 47
Stacy Hotel, 95
Stadium (Barkley Bowl, Jackson), 97, 131
State Board of Education, 112
State forester (Quicksand substation), 144
State Guards: sent to Jackson, 59-60; 69, 95
Stevenson; 145; elevation, 11
Stidham Home, 135, 136
Stidham Hotel, 95
Stidham, J. L., 136
Stidhams, The, 47

164   BREATHITT

Strong-Amis Feud, 58
Strong, Capt. Bill ("Uncle Bill"), 56, 57-58, 61, 62, 64, 65, 68, 70-76; his "firing-squad," 59, 74; joins Little Army, 59; takes over courthouse in Jackson, 59-60; death of, 75-76
Strong-Callahan feud, 70-76
Strong, Ed., 62
Strong, Harlan, viii
Strong, Judge E. C., 61-63
Strong, "Nigger Dick," 64
Strongs, The, 47
Subscription schools, see County and subscription schools
Swan-Day Company, 24
Swift, John, 147
Swinging bridge (Jackson), 97, 132
Synod (Ky.) of the Presbyterian Church, 121

Taulbee, S. E., 16
Taulbees, The, 47
Taxies, xiii
Tennessee Valley Authority, 112
Terry, Charles, viii, 108
Terry, Isaac, 63
Terry, Jackson, 51-52
Terry, Miles, 51
Terries, The, 46
Thacker, Mrs. C. P., viii
Tharp, William, 74
Thomas, W. R., author, 55
Thompson, Ernest Trice, author, 120
Thompson Hotel, 95
Thompson, Lieutenant, 68
Timber, 21-24
Tobacco: 1839 production, 14; 1934 acreage and production, 13
Topography of Breathitt County, 10-11
Tourist information, xiii
Travelers, first, 34-38
Travel and transportation, 27-33
Trees and shrubs, see Flora
Trimble, J. Green, author, 25, 29, 31-32, 51, 84, 85, 99, 100, 104, 118, 120

Troublesome Creek: coal mines, 18; salt works, 25; pioneer settlers, 47
Tunnel, Panhandle, 82
Turner, State Senator Ervine, Jr., 111
Turner, Jesse, E., viii
Turner, Mrs. Marie (Roberts), viii, 111-12, 132
"Turning out the master," 104
Turners, The, 46, 47

United Brethren in Christ, 122, 148
University of Kentucky, 112, 144
Utilities (Jackson), 97

Vancleve Consolidated School, 112
Vancleves, The, 47
Vandermeer, Rev. Samuel, 143
Van Horne, R. M., principal, Breathitt High School, viii, 132
Van Meter, J. O., president, Lees Junior College, viii, 129
Vendettas, 53; see Feuds
Vocational guidance, Breathitt County schools, 112-13

Walker, Sr., surveyor, 35
Watkins', The, 47
Wallace, Judge Caleb, 52
Walters, Laura Fletcher, 139
War between the States: Jackson, 86-87; effect on schools, 103-104; see also Feuds
Warriors' Path, 34
Watts', The, 47
Whitaker, Lick, 95
White, Galen, viii
White, General, 25
Whites, The, 47
Wild flowers, 137-38
Wilhurst, elevation, 11
Wilhurst School, 112
Williams, Mason, 118
Williams, Stephen, 145
Williams', The, 47
Wilson, Alex., 140

Wilsons, The, 47
Wolf Coal, elevation, 11
Wood, A. T. (Dick), 32
Woodson, Silas, 51
Woodworking (Highland Institute), 141

Wool: (1839), 14; today, 17
World War I distinction, 3
Wright, Bill, 84

Yo Hill (Jackson), 86

www.ingramcontent.com/pod-product-compliance
Lightning Source LLC
Chambersburg PA
CBHW030325100526
44592CB00010B/572